HBR Guide to **Finance Basics for Managers**

Harvard Business Review Guides

Arm yourself with the advice you need to succeed on the job, from the most trusted brand in business. Packed with how-to essentials from leading experts, the HBR Guides provide smart answers to your most pressing work challenges.

The titles include:

HBR Guide to Better Business Writing

HBR Guide to Finance Basics for Managers

HBR Guide to Getting the Mentoring You Need

HBR Guide to Getting the Right Job

HBR Guide to Getting the Right Work Done

HBR Guide to Giving Effective Feedback

HBR Guide to Making Every Meeting Matter

HBR Guide to Managing Stress at Work

HBR Guide to Managing Up and Across

HBR Guide to Persuasive Presentations

HBR Guide to Project Management

HBR Guide to **Finance Basics for Managers**

HARVARD BUSINESS REVIEW PRESS

Boston, Massachusetts

Printed in the United States of America

20 19 18 17 16

Library of Congress Cataloging-in-Publication Data

HBR guide to finance basics for managers.
p. cm. — (Harvard business review guides)
ISBN 978-1-4221-8730-2 (alk. paper)
1. Business enterprises—Finance. 2. Financial statements.
I. Harvard business review.
HG4026.H435 2012
658.15—dc23

2012026162

The paper used in this publication meets the requirements of the American National Standard for Permanence of Paper for Publications and Documents in Libraries and Archives z39.48-1992.

What You'll Learn

Where do you begin if your boss asks you to prepare a breakeven analysis? Can you tell the difference between an income statement and a balance sheet? Between gross margin and revenue? Do you understand why a business that's profitable can still go belly-up? Has your grasp of your company's numbers helped—or hurt—your career?

If questions like these make you sweat, you've come to the right place. This guide will give you the tools and confidence you need to master finance basics, as *all* good managers must. You'll learn how to:

- Speak the language of finance
- Compare your firm's financials with rivals'
- Size up your vulnerability to industry downturns
- Shift your unit's focus from revenues to profits
- Use financial data to defend budget requests
- Avoid running out of cash—and going out of business

- Keep costs from killing your bottom line
- Invest smartly through cost/benefit analysis
- Sell your brilliant idea with ROI
- Avoid putting *too* much faith in the numbers

Contents

Section 1
Finance Basics: Don't Be Afraid

"What's the ROI on that software your department wants to buy?"

"The CFO says profits are great but money's tight—everyone needs to conserve cash."

"I've been studying the figures, and it looks as if your sales reps are sacrificing gross margin for revenue. Have you talked to them about that?"

"Our inventory days are creeping upward. We have to find a way to reverse that trend."

"I'm worried about our business. The financials suggest that corporate isn't investing in our future as much as it used to."

Every corporate manager hears questions and comments like these—sometimes from a boss or a finance director, other times from colleagues in water-cooler conversations. Whatever the source, they all have one thing in common: They take for granted that you understand the fundamentals of finance. The people doing the talking presume that you speak the language, that you can read the financial statements, and that you can use basic financial tools to make decisions.

But what if you're not sure of the difference between an income statement and a balance sheet, or between profit and a positive cash flow? What if you can't define inventory days or days sales outstanding, and you don't know how to use those numbers to improve financial performance? If someone asks you to prepare a return on investment (ROI) analysis, do you get a sinking feeling in the pit of your stomach because you have no idea where to begin?

Don't despair.

For one thing, you're in good company. Financial trainers Karen Berman and Joe Knight reported in "Are Your People Financially Literate?" (HBR October 2009) that when their Los Angeles–based Business Literacy Institute administered a 21-question quiz on financial basics to a representative sample of American managers, the average score was only 38%—a failing grade in any classroom. (After you read this introduction, you'll have a chance to quiz yourself with a short sample of similar questions.) At least those managers did better than the group of *Fortune* 500 officers and directors described in Andrew Ross Sorkin's *New York Times* article "Back to School, But This One Is for Top Corporate Officials" (September 3, 2002).

On another, equally basic, test of financial concepts, these executives scored an average of 32%.

But there's another reason not to feel too bad: You can easily remedy your situation. Reading this guide is a great start. The first section introduces you to the key terms and the three main financial statements. The next section shows you how to use some of the essential tools of finance. Learn these, and you'll be able to make better decisions to improve your unit's performance. The final section steps back from the numbers and emphasizes the importance of keeping your wits about you. Finance is partly science, to be sure, but it's also partly an art—and when you apply its tools, you have to be sure you understand the context for what you're doing.

Why bother with all this? The reason is simple: Every business runs on financial data. If you don't know the tools of finance, you can't put that information to work. If you can't even speak the language, you'll be left out of the larger conversation about your company, and your career may suffer as a result. When you finish this guide, you'll be well on your way to understanding and using the tools and the language. You'll also be well positioned to take a couple of advanced courses, so to speak, by turning to sources that dig deeper into the subject.

Do you worry that financial concepts will be too complex or that you won't be able to do the math? Rest assured, learning the fundamentals of finance is not the same as studying to be a numbers pro. People typically go to school for at least a couple of years to become financial experts, and then they spend a lot of time picking up specialized knowledge on the job. This guide won't give you all that—it's just about the basics. And the math involved in using financial tools is relatively simple. Most of the time it's no more complicated than the arithmetic you did in middle school; the stuff that's a little trickier can easily be done on a computer or calculator.

Ready to begin? Take the quiz on the following page. The answers are in the back of the guide, but don't peek yet. Instead, take the quiz again (on page 153) *after* you have read through all the articles, and then compare your two scores. You should be pleased with what you have learned.

Finance Quiz

Do You Know the Basics?

This 10-question quiz isn't designed to measure your entire financial IQ, but it will give you a sense of the fundamentals you should learn to become a more effective manager. When you finish reading the guide, you'll have a chance to retake the quiz and compare your scores. If you don't know an answer, just mark it "don't know" rather than guessing. That will give you a clearer indication of your progress later.

The questions here were developed with the help of the Business Literacy Institute, in Los Angeles. A more comprehensive financial IQ test is available for purchase at www.business-literacy.com.

1. **The income statement measures:**
   a. Profitability
   b. Assets and liabilities
   c. Cash
   d. All of the above

2. **A sale on credit ends up on the income statement as revenue and as what on the balance sheet?**
   a. Accounts receivable
   b. Long-term assets
   c. Short-term liability
   d. Operating cash flow

3. **What happens when a company is profitable but collection lags behind payments to vendors?**
   a. The company is OK because profits always become cash
   b. The company stands a good chance of running out of money
   c. The company needs to shift its focus to EBIT
   d. The cash flow statement will show a negative bottom line

4. **How is gross profit margin calculated?**
   a. COGS/revenue
   b. Gross profit/net profit
   c. Gross profit/revenue
   d. Sales/gross profit

5. **Which statement summarizes changes to parts of the balance sheet?**
   a. Income statement
   b. Cash flow statement
   c. Neither of the above
   d. Both of the above

6. **EBIT is an important measure in companies because:**
   a. It is free cash flow
   b. It subtracts interest and taxes from net income to get a truer picture of the business
   c. It indicates the profitability of a company's operations
   d. It is the key measure of earnings before indirect costs and transfers

7. **Operating expenses include all of the following except:**
   a. Advertising costs
   b. Administrative salaries
   c. Expensed research and development costs
   d. Delivery of raw materials

8. **Owners' equity in a company increases when the company:**
   a. Increases its assets with debt
   b. Decreases its debt by paying off loans with company cash
   c. Increases its profit
   d. All of the above

9. **A company has more cash today when:**
   a. Customers pay their bills sooner
   b. Accounts receivable increases
   c. Profit increases
   d. Retained earnings increases

10. **Which of the following is not part of working capital?**
    a. Accounts receivable
    b. Inventory
    c. Property, plant, and equipment
    d. All of the above are part of working capital

The Key Financial Statements

What does your company own, and what does it owe to others? What are its sources of revenue, and how has it spent its money? How much profit has it made? What is the state of its financial health? You can answer those questions by turning to the three main financial statements: the **balance sheet,** the **income statement,** and the **cash flow statement.**

These are the essential documents of business. Executives use them to assess performance and identify areas for action. Shareholders look at them to keep tabs on how well their capital is being managed. Outside investors use them to identify opportunities. Lenders and suppliers routinely examine them to determine the creditworthiness of the companies with which they deal.

Every manager, no matter where he or she sits in the organization, should have a solid grasp of the basic state-

---

Adapted from *Harvard Business Essentials: Finance for Managers* (product #5788BC), Harvard Business Review Press, 2002

ments. All three follow the same general format from company to company, though specific line items may vary, depending on the nature of the business. If you can, get copies of your own company's most recent financials so that you can compare them with the sample financials discussed here.

The Balance Sheet

Companies prepare balance sheets to summarize their financial position at a given point in time, usually at the end of the month, the quarter, or the fiscal year. The **balance sheet** shows what the company *owns* (its assets), what it *owes* (its liabilities), and its book value, or net worth (also called owners' equity, or shareholders' equity).

Assets comprise all the physical resources a company can put to work in the service of the business. This category includes cash and financial instruments (such as stocks and bonds), inventories of raw materials and finished goods, land, buildings, and equipment, plus the firm's **accounts receivable**—funds owed by customers for goods or services purchased.

Liabilities are debts to suppliers and other creditors. If a firm borrows money from a bank, that's a liability. If it buys $1 million worth of parts—and hasn't paid for those parts as of the date on the balance sheet—that $1 million is a liability. Funds owed to suppliers are known as **accounts payable.**

Owners' equity is what's left after you subtract total liabilities from total assets. A company with $3 million in total assets and $2 million in liabilities has $1 million in owners' equity.

That definition gives rise to what is often called the **fundamental accounting equation:**

$$\text{Assets} - \text{Liabilities} = \text{Owners' Equity}$$

or

$$\text{Assets} = \text{Liabilities} + \text{Owners' Equity}$$

The balance sheet shows assets on one side of the ledger, liabilities and owners' equity on the other. It's called a balance sheet because the two sides must always balance.

Suppose, for example, a computer company acquires $1 million worth of motherboards from an electronic parts supplier, with payment due in 30 days. The purchase increases the company's inventory assets by $1 million and its liabilities—in this case its accounts payable—by an equal amount. The equation stays in balance. Likewise, if the same company were to borrow $100,000 from a bank, the cash infusion would increase both its assets and its liabilities by $100,000.

Now suppose that this company has $4 million in owners' equity, and then $500,000 of uninsured assets burn up in a fire. Though its liabilities remain the same, its owners' equity—what's left after all claims against assets are satisfied—drops to $3.5 million.

Notice how total assets equal total liabilities plus owners' equity in the balance sheet of Amalgamated Hat Rack, an imaginary company whose finances we will consider throughout this chapter. The balance sheet (see page 14) describes not only how much the company has invested in assets but also what kinds of assets it owns, what portion comes from creditors (liabilities), and what portion comes from owners (equity). Analysis of the balance sheet can give you an idea of how efficiently a company is utilizing its assets and managing its liabilities.

Balance sheet data are most helpful when compared with the same information from one or more previous years. Amalgamated Hat Rack's balance sheet shows assets, liabilities, and owners' equity for December 31, 2010, and December 31, 2009. Compare the figures, and you'll see that Amalgamated is moving in a positive direction: It has increased its owners' equity by $397,500.

Now let's take a closer look at each section of the balance sheet.

Assets

Listed first are **current assets:** cash on hand and marketable securities, receivables, and inventory. Generally, current assets can be converted into cash within one year. Next is a tally of **fixed assets,** which are harder to turn into cash. The biggest category of fixed assets is usually **property, plant, and equipment;** for some companies, it's the only category.

Since fixed assets other than land don't last forever, the company must charge a portion of their cost against revenue over their estimated useful life. This is called depreciation, and the balance sheet shows the **accumulated depreciation** for all of the company's fixed assets. Gross property, plant, and equipment minus accumulated depreciation equals the current book value of property, plant, and equipment.

M&A can throw an additional asset category into the mix: If one company has purchased another for a price above the fair market value of its assets, the difference is known as **goodwill,** and it must be recorded. This is an accounting fiction, but goodwill often includes intangibles with real value, such as brand names, intellectual property, or the acquired company's reputation.

Liabilities and owners' equity

Now let's consider the claims against a company's assets. The category **current liabilities** represents money owed to creditors and others that typically must be paid within a year. It includes short-term loans, accrued salaries, accrued income taxes, accounts payable, and the current year's repayment obligation on a long-term loan. **Long-term liabilities** are usually bonds and mortgages—debts that the company is contractually obliged to repay over a period of time longer than a year.

As explained earlier, subtracting total liabilities from total assets leaves owners' equity. Owners' equity includes **retained earnings** (net profits that accumulate on a company's balance sheet after payment of dividends to shareholders) and **contributed capital,** or **paid-in capital** (capital received in exchange for shares).

The balance sheet shows, in effect, how its assets were paid for—from borrowed money (liabilities), the capital of the owners, or both.

Historical Cost

Balance sheet figures may not correspond to actual market values, except for items such as cash, accounts receivable, and accounts payable. This is because accountants must record most items at their historical cost. If, for example, a company's balance sheet indicated land

Amalgamated Hat Rack balance sheet as of December 31, 2010 and 2009

	2010	2009	Increase (Decrease)
Assets			
Cash and marketable securities	$ 652,500	486,500	166,000
Accounts receivable	555,000	512,000	43,000
Inventory	835,000	755,000	80,000
Prepaid expenses	123,000	98,000	25,000
Total current assets	2,165,500	1,851,500	314,000
Gross property, plant, and equipment	2,100,000	1,900,000	200,000
Less: accumulated depreciation	333,000	290,500	(42,500)
Net property, plant, and equipment	1,767,000	1,609,500	157,500
Total assets	$ 3,932,500	3,461,000	471,500
Liabilities and owners' equity			
Accounts payable	$ 450,000	430,000	20,000
Accrued expenses	98,000	77,000	21,000
Income tax payable	17,000	9,000	8,000
Short-term debt	435,000	500,000	(65,000)
Total current liabilities	1,000,000	1,016,000	(16,000)
Long-term debt	750,000	660,000	90,000
Total liabilities	1,750,000	1,676,000	74,000
Contributed capital	900,000	850,000	50,000
Retained earnings	1,282,500	935,000	347,500
Total owners' equity	2,182,500	1,785,000	397,500
Total liabilities and owners' equity	$ 3,932,500	$ 3,461,000	$ 471,500

WHERE ARE THE HUMAN ASSETS?

As people look to financial statements to gain insights about companies, many notice the traditional balance sheet's inability to reflect the value and profit potential of human capital and other intangibles. (Remember that the intangibles included in goodwill appear only when one company acquires another, and that the figure represents only the acquiree's intangibles at the time of purchase.) The absence of intangibles from the balance sheet is particularly significant for knowledge-intensive companies, whose skills, intellectual property, brand equity, and customer relationships may be their most productive assets. Indeed, a study several years ago by Baruch Lev of New York University found that 40% of the market valuation of the average company was missing from its balance sheet. For high-tech firms, the figure was over 50%. So managers and investors must look beyond the bricks and mortar, the equipment, and the cash that constitute balance sheet assets to determine the real value of a company.

worth $700,000, that figure would be what the company paid for the land way back when. If it was purchased in downtown San Francisco in 1960, you can bet that it is now worth immensely more than the value stated on the balance sheet. So why do accountants use historical instead of market values? The short answer is that it's the lesser of two evils. If market values were required, then every public company would be required to get a professional appraisal of every one of its properties, warehouse inventories, and so forth, and would have to do so every year—a logistical nightmare.

How the Balance Sheet Relates to You

Though the balance sheet is prepared by accountants, it's filled with important information for nonfinancial managers. Later in this guide you'll learn how to use balance-sheet ratios in managing your own area. For the moment, let's just look at a couple of ways in which balance-sheet figures indicate how efficiently a company is operating.

Working capital

Subtracting current liabilities from current assets gives you the company's **net working capital,** or the amount of money tied up in current operations. A quick calculation from its most recent balance sheet shows that Amalgamated had $1,165,500 in net working capital at the end of 2010.

Financial managers give substantial attention to the level of working capital, which typically expands and contracts with the level of sales. Too little working capital can put a company in a bad position: It may be unable to pay its bills or take advantage of profitable opportunities. But too much working capital reduces profitability since that capital must be financed in some way, usually through interest-bearing loans.

Inventory is a component of working capital that directly affects many nonfinancial managers. As with working capital in general, there's a tension between having too much and too little. On the one hand, plenty of inventory solves business problems. The company can fill customer orders without delay, and the inventory provides a buffer against potential production stoppages or interruptions in the flow of raw materials or parts. On the other hand, every piece of inventory must be financed, and the market value of the inventory itself may decline while it sits on the shelf.

The early years of the personal computer business provided a dramatic example of how excess inventory can wreck the bottom line. Some analysts estimated that the value of finished-goods inventory—computers that had already been built—melted away at a rate of approximately 2% *per day,* because of technical obsolescence in this fast-moving industry. Inventory meltdown really hammered Apple during the mid-1990s. Until the company could dramatically reduce its inventories through operational redesign, it had to dump its obsolete components and finished goods onto the market at huge discounts. By comparison, its rival, Dell, built computers to order—so it operated with *no* finished-goods inventory and with relatively small stocks of components. Dell's success formula was an ultrafast supply chain and assembly system that enabled the company to build PCs to customers' specifications. Finished Dell PCs didn't end up on stockroom shelves for weeks at a time, but went directly from the assembly line into waiting delivery trucks. The profit lesson to managers in this kind of situation is clear: Shape your operations to minimize inventories.

Financial leverage

The use of borrowed money to acquire an asset is called **financial leverage.** People say that a company is highly leveraged when the percentage of debt on its balance sheet is high relative to the capital invested by the owners. (**Operating leverage,** in contrast, refers to the extent to which a company's operating costs are fixed rather than variable. For example, a company that relies on heavy investments in machinery and very few workers to produce its goods has a high operating leverage.)

Financial leverage can increase returns on an investment, but it also increases risk. For example, suppose that you paid $400,000 for an asset, using $100,000 of your own money and $300,000 in borrowed funds. For simplicity, we'll ignore loan payments, taxes, and any cash flow you might get from the investment. Four years go by, and your asset has appreciated to $500,000. Now you decide to sell. After paying off the $300,000 loan, you end up with $200,000 in your pocket—your original $100,000 plus a $100,000 profit. That's a gain of 100% on your personal capital, even though the asset increased in value by only 25%. Financial leverage made this possible. If you had financed the purchase entirely with your own funds ($400,000), you would have ended up with only a 25% gain. In the United States and most other countries, tax policy makes financial leverage even more attractive by allowing businesses to treat the interest paid on loans as a deductible business expense.

But leverage can cut both ways. If the value of an asset drops, or if it fails to produce the anticipated level of revenue, then leverage works against the asset's owner. Consider what would have happened in our example if the asset's value had dropped by $100,000—that is, to $300,000. The owner would still have to repay the initial loan of $300,000 and would have nothing left over. The entire $100,000 investment would have disappeared.

Financial structure of the firm

The negative potential of financial leverage is what keeps CEOs, their financial executives, and board members from maximizing their companies' debt financing. Instead, they seek a financial structure that creates a realistic balance between debt and equity on the balance sheet. Although leverage enhances a company's potential profitability as long as things go right, managers know that every dollar of debt increases risk, both because of the danger just cited and because high debt entails high interest costs, which must be paid in good times and bad. Many companies have failed when business reversals or recessions reduced their ability to make timely payments on their loans.

When creditors and investors examine corporate balance sheets, therefore, they look carefully at the debt-to-equity ratio. They factor the riskiness of the balance sheet into the interest they charge on loans and the return they demand from a company's bonds. A highly leveraged company, for example, may have to pay two or three times the interest rate paid by a less leveraged competitor. Investors also demand a higher rate of return for their stock investments in highly leveraged companies. They will not accept high risks without expecting commensurately large returns.

The Income Statement

Unlike the balance sheet, which is a snapshot of a company's position at one point in time, the **income statement** shows cumulative business results within a defined time frame, such as a quarter or a year. It tells you whether the company is making a profit or a loss—that is, whether it has positive or negative net income (net earnings)—and how much. This is why the income statement is often referred to as the **profit-and-loss statement,** or **P&L.** The income statement also tells you the company's revenues and expenses during the time period it covers. Knowing the revenues and the profit enables you to determine the company's **profit margin.**

As we did with the balance sheet, we can represent the contents of the income statement with a simple equation:

$$\text{Revenues} - \text{Expenses} = \text{Net Income}$$

An income statement starts with the company's **sales,** or **revenues.** This is primarily the value of the goods or services delivered to customers, but you may have revenues from other sources as well. Note that revenues in most cases are not the same as cash. If a company delivers $1 million worth of goods in December 2010 and sends out an invoice at the end of the month, for example, that $1 million in sales counts as revenue for the year 2010 even though the customer hasn't yet paid the bill.

Various expenses—the costs of making and storing a company's goods, administrative costs, depreciation of plant and equipment, interest expense, and taxes—are then deducted from revenues. The bottom line—what's left over—is the **net income** (or **net profit,** or **net earnings**) for the period covered by the statement.

Let's look at the various line items on the income statement for Amalgamated Hat Rack (see below). The **cost of goods sold,** or **COGS,** represents the direct costs of manufacturing hat racks. This figure covers raw materials, such as lumber, and everything needed to turn those materials into finished goods, such as labor. Subtracting cost of goods sold from revenues gives us Amalgamated's **gross profit**—an important measure of a company's financial performance. In 2010, gross profit was $1,600,000.

Amalgamated Hat Rack income statement

	For the period ending December 31, 2010
Retail sales	$ 2,200,000
Corporate sales	1,000,000
Total sales revenue	3,200,000
Less: Cost of goods sold	1,600,000
Gross profit	1,600,000
Less: Operating expenses	800,000
Less: Depreciation expenses	42,500
Earnings before interest and taxes	757,500
Less: Interest expense	110,000
Earnings before income taxes	647,500
Less: Income taxes	300,000
Net income	$ 347,500

The next major category of cost is **operating expenses,** which include the salaries of administrative employees, office rents, sales and marketing costs, and other costs not directly related to making a product or delivering a service.

Depreciation appears on the income statement as an expense, even though it involves no out-of-pocket payment. As described earlier, it's a way of allocating the cost of an asset over the asset's estimated useful life. A truck, for example, might be expected to last five years. The company wouldn't count the full cost of the truck as an expense on the income statement in the first year; it would depreciate that amount over the full five years.

Subtracting operating expenses and depreciation from gross profit gives you a company's **operating earnings,** or **operating profit.** This is often called **earnings before interest and taxes,** or **EBIT,** as it is on Amalgamated's statement.

The last expenses on the income statement are typically taxes and any interest due on loans. If you get a positive net profit figure after subtracting all expenses, as Amalgamated does, your company is profitable.

Multiyear Comparisons

As with the balance sheet, comparing income statements over a period of years reveals much more than examining a single income statement. You can spot trends, turnarounds, and recurring problems. Many companies' annual reports show data going back five or more years.

In Amalgamated's multiperiod income statement (see page 25), you can see that annual retail sales have grown steadily, while corporate sales have declined slightly. Operating expenses have stayed about the same, however, even as total sales have expanded. That's a good sign that management is holding the line on the cost of doing business. Interest expense has also declined, perhaps because the company has paid off one of its loans. The bottom line, net income, shows healthy growth.

How the Income Statement Relates to You

Of the three main financial statements, the income statement generally has the greatest bearing on a manager's job. That's because most managers are responsible in some way for one or more of its elements:

Generating revenue

In one sense, nearly everyone in a company helps generate revenue—the people who design and produce the goods or deliver the service, those who deal directly with customers, and so on—but it's the primary responsibility of the sales and marketing departments. If same-store or same-product revenues rise faster than the competition's, you can reasonably assume that the folks in sales and marketing are doing a good job.

It's critical that managers in these departments understand the income statement so that they can balance costs against revenue. If sales reps give too many discounts, for instance, they may reduce the company's gross profit. If marketers spend too much money in pursuit of new customers, they will eat into operating profit. It's the manager's job to track these numbers as well as revenue itself.

Managing budgets

Running a department means working within the confines of a budget. If you oversee a unit in information technology or human resources, for example, you may have little influence on revenue, but you will surely be expected to watch your costs closely—and all those costs will affect the income statement. Staff departments' expenses usually show up in the operating expenses line. If you invest in any capital equipment—a complex piece of software, say—you will also add to the depreciation line.

Close study of your company's income statements over time reveals opportunities as well as constraints. Suppose you would like to get permission to hire one or two more people. If operating expense as a percentage of sales has been trending downward, you will have a stronger case than if it has been trending upward.

Managing a P&L

Many managers have P&L responsibility, which means they are accountable for an entire chunk of the income statement. This is probably the case if you're running a business unit, a store, a plant, or a branch office, or if you're overseeing a product line. The income statement you are accountable for isn't quite the same as the whole company's. For instance, it is unlikely to include interest expense and other overhead items, except as an "allocation" at the end of the year. Even so, your job is to manage revenue generation and costs so that your unit or product line contributes as much profit to the company as pos-

Amalgamated Hat Rack multiperiod income statement

	For the period ending December 31,		
	2010	2009	2008
Retail sales	$ 2,200,000	2,000,000	1,720,000
Corporate sales	1,000,000	1,000,000	1,100,000
Total sales revenue	3,200,000	3,000,000	2,820,000
Less: Cost of goods sold	1,600,000	1,550,000	1,400,000
Gross profit	1,600,000	1,450,000	1,420,000
Less: Operating expenses	800,000	810,000	812,000
Less: Depreciation expenses	42,500	44,500	45,500
Earnings before interest and taxes	757,500	595,500	562,500
Less: Interest expense	110,000	110,000	150,000
Earnings before income taxes	647,500	485,500	412,500
Less: Income taxes	300,000	194,200	165,000
Net income	$ 347,500	291,300	247,500

sible. For that you need to understand and track revenue, cost of goods sold, and operating expenses.

The Cash Flow Statement

The **cash flow statement** is the least used—and least understood—of the three essential statements. It shows in broad categories how a company acquired and spent its cash during a given span of time. As you'd expect, expenditures show up on the statement as negative figures, and sources of income figures are positive. The bottom line in each category is simply the net total of inflows and outflows, and it can be either positive or negative.

The statement has three major categories: **Operating activities,** or **operations,** refers to cash generated by, and used in, a company's ordinary business operations. It includes everything that doesn't explicitly fall into the other two categories. **Investing activities** covers cash spent on capital equipment and other investments (outgoing), and cash realized from the sale of such investments (incoming). **Financing activities** refers to cash used to reduce debt, buy back stock, or pay dividends

Amalgamated Hat Rack cash flow statement for the year ending December 31, 2010

Net income	$ 347,500
Operating activities	
Accounts receivable	(43,000)
Inventory	(80,000)
Prepaid expenses	(25,000)
Accounts payable	20,000
Accrued expenses	21,000
Income tax payable	8,000
Depreciation expense	42,500
Total changes in operating assets and liabilities	(56,500)
Cash flow from operations	291,000
Investing activities	
Sale of property, plant, and equipment	267,000*
Capital expenditures	(467,000)
Cash flow from investing activities	(200,000)
Financing activities	
Short-term debt decrease	(65,000)
Long-term borrowing	90,000
Capital stock	50,000
Cash dividends to stockholders	–
Cash flow from financing activities	75,000
Increase in cash during year	$ 166,000

* Assumes sale price was at book value; the company had yet to start depreciating this asset.

(outgoing), and cash from loans or from stock sales (incoming).

Again using the Amalgamated Hat Rack example, we see that in 2010 the company generated a total positive cash flow (increase in cash) of $166,000. This is the sum of cash flows from operations ($291,000), investing activities (minus $200,000), and financing ($75,000).

The cash flow statement shows the relationship between net profit, from the income statement, and the actual change in cash that appears in the company's bank accounts. In accounting language, it "reconciles" profit and cash through a series of adjustments to net profit. Some of these adjustments are simple. Depreciation, for instance, is a noncash expense, so you have to add depreciation to net profit if what you're interested in is the change in cash. Other adjustments are harder to grasp, though the arithmetic isn't difficult. If a company's accounts receivable are lower at the end of 2010 than they were at the end of 2009, for example, it took in "extra" cash from operations, so we would add that to net profit as well.

Let's look at each category on Amalgamated's cash flow statement for 2010.

- **Operating activities.** Net income—$347,500—appears at the top. That's the figure we want to adjust, and it comes straight from the bottom line of the income statement. Accounts receivable, inventory, prepaid expenses, accounts payable, accrued expenses, and income tax payable are all calculated from the balance sheets for 2010 and

2009. The figure appearing on the cash flow statement for each line item represents the *difference* between the two balance sheets. Again, these are all adjustments that will help translate net income into cash. As mentioned, depreciation is a non-cash expense, so it's added in. Then all the pluses and minuses are calculated to get net cash from operations.

- **Investing activities.** Amalgamated sold fixed assets—property, plant, and equipment—worth $267,000 in 2010. For simplicity's sake we're assuming that it had not yet begun to depreciate those assets. It also invested $467,000 in new fixed assets.

- **Financing activities.** Amalgamated decreased its short-term debt by $65,000, increased its long-term debt by $90,000, and sold $50,000 in stock to investors. It paid its shareholders no dividends in 2010; if it had, the amount would have shown up under financing activities.

- **Change in cash.** As noted above, the change in cash is just the total of all three categories. It corresponds exactly to the difference in the cash line items on the balance sheets for 2010 and 2009.

The cash flow statement is useful because it indicates whether your company is successfully turning its profits into cash—and that ability is ultimately what will keep the company **solvent,** or able to pay bills as they come due.

How the Cash Flow Statement Relates to You

If you're a manager in a large corporation, changes in your employer's cash flow won't typically have an impact on your day-to-day job. Nevertheless, it's a good idea to stay up to date with your company's cash situation, because it may affect your budget for the upcoming year. When cash is tight, you will probably want to be conservative in your planning. When it's plentiful, you may have an opportunity to propose a bigger budget. Note that a company can be quite profitable and still be short of cash as a result of making a lot of new investments, for example, or having trouble collecting receivables.

You may also have some influence over the items that affect the cash flow statement. Are you responsible for inventory? Keep in mind that every addition there requires a cash expenditure. Are you in sales? A sale isn't really a sale until it is paid for—so watch your receivables. There's more on tools for managing cash later in this guide.

Where to Find the Financials

Every company with shares traded in U.S. public financial markets must prepare and distribute its financial statements in an annual report to shareholders. Annual reports usually go beyond the basic disclosure requirement of the Securities and Exchange Commission and include discussion of the year's operations and the future outlook. Most public companies also issue quarterly reports.

If you are looking for even more material on your company, or on one of your competitors, obtain a copy of its annual Form 10-K. The 10-K often contains abundant and revealing information about a company's strategy, its view of the market and its customers, its products, its important risks and business challenges, and so forth. You can get 10-K reports and annual and quarterly reports directly from a company's investor relations department or online at www.sec.gov/edgar/searchedgar/webusers.htm.

Private, or closely held, companies are not required by law to share full financial statements with anybody, though prospective investors and lenders naturally expect to see all three statements. And many companies share the financials with their managers. If you work for a closely held company and have not seen its financials, ask someone in finance whether you are allowed to see them.

SUMMING UP

The balance sheet, income statement, and cash flow statement offer three perspectives on a company's financial performance. They tell three different but related stories about how well your company is doing financially:

- The **balance sheet** shows a company's financial position at a specific point in time. It provides a snapshot of its assets, liabilities, and equity on a given day.
- The **income statement** shows the bottom line. It indicates how much profit or loss was generated over a period of time—usually a month, a quarter, or a year.
- The **cash flow statement** tells where the company's cash came from and where it went. It shows the relationship between net profit and the change in cash recorded from one balance sheet to the next.

Together, these financial statements can help you understand what is going on in your company—or in any other business.

The Fundamental Laws of Business

by David Stauffer

Why was a publisher willing to pay General Electric chairman Jack Welch an eye-popping $7 million advance for a book about his career? According to Dallas-based management consultant Ram Charan, author of *What the CEO Wants You to Know* and several other books, the answer has a lot to do with Welch's ability to distill complexities—to think and talk about his sprawling global conglomerate as if it were a simple street-corner shop. An understanding of a few financial measures coupled with an enterprise-wide perspective, Charan maintains, can help you get a grip on any company, regardless of its size or location. "When you come right down to it," he says, "business is very simple. There are universal laws of

---

Adapted from *Harvard Management Update* (product #U0104A), April 2001

business that apply whether you sell fruit from a stand or are running a *Fortune* 500 company."

Understand the Measures of Moneymaking

Business acumen, writes Charan, is "the ability to understand the building blocks of how a one-person operation or a very big business makes money." Problems arise when managers don't have a precise understanding of what "making money" means. Three measures can give you a good picture of whether and how a company is making money: growth, cash generation, and return on assets.

Growth

Growth in sales is usually—but not always—a positive sign. A $16 million injection-molding company, writes Charan, "rewarded its sales representatives based on how many dollars' worth of plastic caps they sold, regardless of whether the company made a profit on the caps. Everyone was excited when the company landed $4 million in new sales from two major customers. But in the following three years, as sales rose, profit margins sank." The lesson here: "Growth for its own sake doesn't do any good. Growth has to be profitable and sustainable."

Cash generation

Cash is "a company's oxygen supply," writes Charan; it "gives you the ability to stay in business." Even if your company is growing its revenues profitably and getting a respectable return on its assets, a cash shortage—or a declining cash flow—spells trouble. "Cash generation is

BIG-PICTURE PERSPECTIVE

Consultant Ram Charan, author of *What the CEO Wants You to Know*, urges you to "get a total picture" by answering the following questions:

- What were your company's sales during the last year? Are sales growing, declining, or flat?
- What is the profit margin? Is it growing, declining, or flat?
- How does your margin compare with those of competitors? With those of other industries?
- Do you know your company's inventory velocity? Its asset velocity?
- What is its return on assets?
- Is cash generation increasing or decreasing? Why?
- Is your company gaining or losing against the competition?

the difference between all the cash that flows into the business and all the cash that flows out of the business in a given time period," Charan explains. Since most companies extend and receive credit, net cash flow and profit are seldom the same thing. Cash from operations depends largely on two factors: **accounts receiv-**

able (money owed by customers) and **accounts payable** (money owed to suppliers).

Charan recommends continually investigating where the cash is being generated, how it's being used, and whether enough is coming in. If there's not enough, of course, you'll want to find out the reasons.

Return on assets (ROA)

A company's ROA is its net profit divided by the average value of its assets during a given period of time. This measure, usually expressed as a percentage, shows you how well your company is using its assets—including cash, receivables, inventory, buildings, vehicles, and machinery—to make money. ROA gives managers a glimpse of the often-missing third element of a triad called SEA: sales, expenses, and assets. "Below the senior management level," explains Chuck Kremer, a financial trainer and coauthor of *Managing by the Numbers,* "many decision makers see only their part of the income statement," which doesn't deal with assets. Yet all employees, whether they realize it or not, are involved in managing some portion of the firm's assets.

Many people equate managing assets with watching gross profit (total sales minus all costs directly associated with creating the company's products or services). That's only half the challenge, says Charan. The other measure that needs to be monitored simultaneously is **velocity**—how fast a particular asset moves "through a business to a customer."

In times of intense price competition, for example, companies often see their gross margins shrink. Increasing asset velocity helps protect the ROA of a company in that situation, because you're doing more with fewer assets. This is the strategy that made Dell Computer so successful in the 1990s. By outsourcing much of its components manufacturing, Dell essentially became an assembler, Charan points out: Each computer was configured to meet an individual customer's specifications and delivered in less than a week. Dell cut costs by reducing inventory and increasing its **inventory turns**—the number of times in a year that its inventory turned over—to a level far higher than most manufacturers'.

"The problem with managers missing the 'A,' or assets part [of SEA], isn't usually apparent in good times," Kremer says. "It's when things are slowing down that ROA makes all the difference. And it's the companies like GE that emphasize the 'A' continuously—so that their people are always managing the receivables, the fixed assets, and the inventories—that thrive in good times and bad."

Think Like an Owner

By understanding growth, cash generation, and ROA, managers can counteract the common tendency to think and act within one's "silo" (department or unit). "None of us denies that we're members of a team comprising every department," Kremer says. "But how can I best contribute to the team if I don't understand how my actions in marketing impact engineering or production?"

Tracking these financial measures helps expand managers' thinking in three ways, says Charan: "First, we're able to think of the business as a whole. Second, we see the linkages between our unit and the business as a whole.

Third, we're better able to grasp what's happening in the outside world—such as an economic slowdown—and relate that to the company and even to our own area."

A big-picture understanding of basic financial measures has very practical benefits, says Thomas Kroeger, the executive vice president in charge of organization and people at Office Depot. "The main benefit is that it helps us cut through the clutter," he says, noting that Office Depot's fast growth necessarily created layers and distance between the CEO and store managers. Kroeger describes a telling incident that occurred during a meeting of district store managers, who had suggested that each store hire a customer greeter. At the individual store level, this didn't represent a huge financial commitment. But when the managers took a step back, they realized that their idea would cost $25 million annually to execute. "They were dumbfounded," Kroeger recalls. "But they'd experienced a critical shift, from the perspective of store manager to store *owner*."

At Alcoa Packaging Machinery in Englewood, Colorado, a financial-literacy initiative helped foster an owner's perspective among all employees. "Workers in each of about 10 manufacturing cells make the decisions that affect *them*," explains machinists' union representative Garry Harper. Should we work this Saturday? Should we buy the new tooling we need this month? The company's big picture gets factored into the decision making around such questions. What's more, all employees receive monthly updates on key financial measures of companywide performance at cell briefings and via the company's intranet. "Every cell also gets its own monthly

P&L statement," Harper adds. "I can assure you that every employee knows or has access to how well his or her cell is contributing to overall company performance."

Growth, cash generation, and return on assets—these concepts, along with a focus on customers, form the nucleus from which everything else about a business emanates, says Charan.

David Stauffer heads the corporate writing firm Stauffer Bury, in Red Lodge, Montana.

Section 2
Making Good Decisions—and Moving Those Numbers

Part of your job as a manager is to help your company reach its financial goals—in other words, to help move the key numbers in the right direction. You should now have a good idea of what those numbers are. The **income statement** shows revenue, the various costs and expenses, subtotals such as gross profit and operating profit, and of course the bottom line—net profit. The **balance sheet** shows assets and liabilities, including accounts receivable and accounts payable. The **cash flow statement** shows how well the company is turning its profits into cash and what it's doing with that cash. All three statements reflect the daily actions of managers and employees throughout the organization. The company will be financially healthy if and only if those individuals make and execute good decisions every day.

The articles in this section of the guide will help you do that. They'll enable you to see more of what the financials are telling you, where the levers and pressure points are, and what you can do to make those key numbers move. You'll learn how to help boost profits, how to use assets (such as equipment, inventory, and cash) more efficiently, how to improve your company's cash flow, and how to analyze potential investments. You'll have a better understanding of the relationship between your responsibilities and your company's financial results.

If you're a savvy manager, you always pay careful attention to the operations you oversee and to the people on your team. But you can't forget that you and your coworkers are ultimately responsible for your company's financial health—and that you must watch the numbers as closely as you watch everything else.

Using Statements to Measure Financial Health

By themselves, financial statements tell you quite a bit: how much profit the company made, where it spent its money, how large its debts are. But how do you *interpret* all the numbers these statements provide? For example, is the company's profit large or small? Is the level of debt healthy or not?

Ratio analysis allows you to dig into the information contained in the three financial statements. A financial ratio is just two key numbers expressed in relation to each other. Using ratios, you can compare your company's performance to that of its competitors, to industry averages, and to its own performance in the past. The ratios that follow are among the most common, and are used in many different industries.

Adapted from *Pocket Mentor: Understanding Finance* (product #13197), Harvard Business Review Press, 2007

Profitability Ratios

These measures gauge a company's **profitability**—its profits as a percentage of various other numbers. They'll help you determine whether your company's profits are healthy or anemic, and whether they're moving in the right direction.

- **Return on assets (ROA).** ROA indicates how well a company is using its assets to generate profit. It's a good measure for comparing companies of different sizes. To calculate it, just divide net income by total assets. For example, look back at the financials of Amalgamated Hat Rack in "The Key Financial Statements," in the opening section of this guide. The income statement shows net income of $347,500 for 2010, and the balance sheet shows total assets of $3,932,500 for December 31 of that year. Do the arithmetic, and you find that Amalgamated's ROA is 8.8%.
- **Return on equity (ROE).** ROE shows profit as a percentage of shareholders' equity. In effect, it's the owners' return on their investment—and you can bet that shareholders will be comparing it to what they could earn with alternative investments. To calculate ROE, divide net income by owners' equity. For Amalgamated, it's $347,500 divided by $2,182,500, or 15.9%.
- **Return on sales (ROS).** Also known as **net profit margin,** ROS measures how well a company is controlling its costs and turning revenue into

bottom-line profit. To calculate ROS, divide net income by revenue. Amalgamated's ROS for 2010 is 10.9%, or $347,500 divided by $3,200,000. For 2009, the calculation is $291,300 divided by $3,000,000, or 9.7%. So Amalgamated's ROS is growing—a very good sign.

- **Gross profit margin.** Gross profit margin shows how efficiently a company produces its goods or delivers its services, taking only direct costs into account. To calculate gross profit margin, divide gross profit by revenue. Amalgamated made $1,600,000 in gross profit in 2010; divide that by $3,200,000, and you get exactly 50%. That's a couple of percentage points higher than the previous year's gross profit margin—also a good sign.

- **Earnings before interest and taxes (EBIT) margin.** Many analysts use this measure, also known as **operating margin,** to see how profitable a company's overall operations are, without regard to how they are financed or what taxes the company may be liable for. To calculate it, just divide EBIT by revenue. Amalgamated's EBIT for 2010 was $757,500. Divide that by revenue, and you get 23.7%. (For an exercise, check to see whether its EBIT margin improved since 2009.)

Operating Ratios

Operating ratios help you assess a company's level of efficiency—in particular, how well it is putting its assets to work and managing its cash.

- **Asset turnover.** This ratio shows how efficiently a company uses all of its assets—cash, machinery, and so on—to generate revenue. It answers the question, *How many dollars of revenue do we bring in for each dollar of assets?* To calculate asset turnover, divide revenue by total assets. In general, the higher the number, the better—but note that you can raise the ratio either by generating more revenue with the same assets *or* by decreasing the asset base of your business, perhaps by lowering average receivables.

- **Receivable days.** This measure, also known as **days sales outstanding (DSO),** tells you how quickly a company collects funds owed by customers. A company that takes an average of 45 days to collect its receivables will need significantly more working capital than one that takes 25 days. There are a couple of different ways to calculate DSO. One common method is to divide ending accounts receivable—accounts receivable on the last day of the month or year—by revenue per day during the period just ended.

- **Days payable.** This measure, also called **days payable outstanding (DPO),** tells you how quickly a company pays its suppliers. The longer it takes, other things being equal, the more cash a company has to work with. Of course, you have to balance the advantages of more cash in your bank account against your suppliers' need to be paid—stretch DPO out too long, and you may find that suppliers don't want to do business with you. The most common way to calculate DPO is to divide ending accounts payable by cost of goods sold per day.

- **Days in inventory (DII).** This shows how quickly a company sells its inventory during a given period of time. The longer it takes, the longer the company's cash is tied up and the greater the likelihood that the inventory will not sell at full value. To calculate DII, or **inventory days,** divide average inventory by cost of goods sold per day.

Liquidity Ratios

Liquidity ratios tell you about a company's ability to meet short-term financial obligations such as debt payments, payroll, and accounts payable.

- **Current ratio.** This ratio measures a company's current assets against its current liabilities. To calculate it, divide total current assets by total current liabilities. A ratio that is close to 1 is too low: It shows that current assets are barely sufficient to cover short-term obligations. (A ratio of less than 1 is a sign of immediate trouble.) A ratio significantly higher than industry averages may indicate that the company is too "fat"—in other words, that it's holding a lot of cash that it's not putting to work or returning to shareholders in the form of dividends.
- **Quick ratio.** This ratio isn't faster to compute than any other—it simply measures a company's abil-

ity to meet its current obligations quickly. It thus ignores inventory, which can be hard to liquidate. (And if you do have to liquidate inventory quickly, you typically get less for it than you would otherwise.) This ratio is sometimes called the **acid test,** because if it is less than 1 the company may be unable to pay its bills. To calculate the quick ratio, divide current assets minus inventory by current liabilities.

Leverage Ratios

Leverage ratios tell you to what extent a company is using debt to pay for its operations and how easily it can cover the cost of that debt.

- **Interest coverage.** This ratio assesses the margin of safety on a company's debt—in other words, how its profit compares to its interest payments during a given period. To calculate interest coverage, divide earnings before interest and taxes by interest expense. For Amalgamated Hat Rack, it's $757,500 divided by $110,000, or 6.9. Bankers and other lenders look at this ratio closely; nobody likes to lend money to a company if its profits aren't substantially higher than its interest obligations.

- **Debt to equity.** This measure shows the extent to which a company is using borrowed money to enhance the return on owners' equity. Investors and lenders scrutinize the ratio to determine whether a company is too highly leveraged (usually compared to industry averages)—or whether, in contrast, management has been too conservative and isn't using enough debt to generate profits. To calculate it, divide total liabilities by owners' equity. Amalgamated's debt-to-equity ratio? It's $1,750,000 divided by $2,182,500, or 0.80.

How Ratio Analysis Relates to You

Ratios shine a powerful light on three potential areas of concern:

- **Liquidity.** The current and quick ratios can tell you whether a company will be able to pay its bills. If it can't easily do so, it's likely to cut costs abruptly. It may even need to restructure its operations.

- **Competitive advantages or disadvantages.** Comparing a company's ratios to those of competitors and to industry averages often reveals specific financial strengths and weaknesses. If your firm's debt-to-equity ratio is higher than average, for example, the company may be particularly vulnerable to a downturn in the industry. If its EBIT margin is higher than competitors', it may be more efficient than others in its operating processes.

- **Performance trends.** If ROS is shrinking, say—if costs are growing relative to sales—senior executives will probably begin looking for cuts. They'll ask managers to tighten their budgets, maybe even to delay hiring where possible. A growing ROA or ROS, by contrast, may put the senior team in a more expansive mood. That's the best time to consider asking for a more generous budget, a new position in your department, or a new piece of capital equipment.

It's important to understand which ratios you can influence and to talk with your team about how to have the right impact. For instance:

Profitability ratios

Most line managers are directly responsible for controlling costs in their areas. By staying under budget, for example, you can help your company's ROS. There may be other ways to improve profitability as well. If you're in engineering or product development, can you come up with new product ideas that will generate additional revenue at healthy margins? If you're in sales, are you watching the gross profit on what you and your team sell as well as your overall sales volume? If you're in marketing, can you figure out ways to get more bang from every marketing dollar? These are the kinds of efforts that make a bottom-line difference.

Operating ratios

Line managers influence operating ratios in a number of ways. Sales managers, for example, always have to make certain that their reps aren't selling to too many customers that are poor credit risks. They may need to work with their reps and the credit department to keep receivable days down to an appropriate level. Plant managers and everyone else responsible for inventory must watch inventory days relative to competitors' and to industry averages. Inventory that's higher than necessary requires more working capital, and the finance department is likely to come around asking why DII is so high.

Liquidity and leverage ratios

These ratios are mostly the responsibility of the finance department, so line managers have less influence on them. But all the other moves discussed here—generating more revenue, watching costs and profit margins, collecting on receivables, keeping inventory (and thus working capital) to a minimum—will ultimately have a positive impact on your company's liquidity and leverage ratios.

Other Financial Assessments

Other ways of evaluating a company's financial health include valuation, Economic Value Added (EVA), and productivity assessments. Like the ratios described above, all these measures are most meaningful when compared with the same ones from earlier time periods or with those for other companies in a particular industry.

Valuation

Valuation often refers to the process of determining the total value of a company for the purpose of selling it. This is an uncertain science. For example, a company considering an acquisition might estimate the prospective acquiree's future cash flows and then calculate its value accordingly. Another would-be acquirer might rely on

TIPS ON ANALYZING FINANCIAL STATEMENTS

- ***Compare companies to determine the context.*** What looks like a big (or small) number may not be once you understand what's typical for a similar-sized business in the same industry. For instance, the oil company ConocoPhillips earned close to $5 billion in 2010, which sounds like a lot of money. But the company's ROS was only 3.5%, compared with 6.4% for Chevron, which recorded only moderately higher revenue.
- ***Watch for trends.*** How have the statements changed since last year? From three years ago? Say you notice a marked increase in the level of receivables from one year to the next. To see whether it's "really" rising, calculate receivable days. If that's going up, too, then the company isn't doing as good a job at collecting its cash as it did in the past. That may be a deliberate

different data, such as the value of the acquiree's physical assets. Regardless of the method used, a company may be worth different amounts to different parties. A small high-tech firm, for instance, may be valued well beyond what its cash flow or assets would suggest if the potential acquirer wants its unique technology or engineering talent.

Valuation also refers to the process by which Wall Street investors and analysts scrutinize financial statements and stock performance to arrive at an estimate

strategy of buying market share, or it may simply reflect poor management of receivables.

- ***Translate the numbers into prose.*** Use your company's statements to write a paragraph describing how much profit it is making, how well it is managing its assets, where the money comes from, and where it goes. If you worked for Amalgamated Hat Rack, for instance, you might begin with, "We've done a pretty good job at increasing revenue over the years, and we've done a very good job of controlling our costs, particularly in 2010. That has helped boost our operating profit and our net profit as well." If you can put what you see on the statements into everyday language, you'll be able to use what the statements are telling you to make smart decisions.

of a company's value. They're interested in determining whether the market price of a share of stock is a good deal relative to the underlying value of the piece of the company that the share represents.

Wall Street uses various means of valuation—that is, of assessing a company's financial health in relation to its stock price:

- **Earnings per share (EPS)** equals net income divided by the number of shares outstanding. This is one of the most commonly watched financial indicators. If it falls, it will most likely take the stock's price down with it.

- **Price-to-earnings ratio (P/E)** is the current price of a share of stock divided by the previous 12 months' earnings per share. It is a common measure of how cheap or expensive a share is relative to the company's earnings (and relative to other companies' shares).

- **Growth indicators** are also important in Wall Street's valuations, because growth allows a company to provide increasing returns to its shareholders. The number of years over which you should measure growth depends on the industry's business cycles. For an oil company, a one-year growth figure probably wouldn't tell you much, because of the industry's long cycles. For an internet company, however, a year is a long time. Typical measures include sales growth, profitability growth, and growth in earnings per share.

Economic Value Added

This concept encourages employees and managers to think like shareholders and owners by focusing on the **net value** a company creates. EVA is the profit remaining after the company has accounted for the cost of its capital. If profit is less than the cost of capital—that is, if EVA is negative—the company is essentially destroying value.

Productivity measures

Sales per employee and net income per employee link revenue and profit-generation information to workforce data. Trend lines in these numbers help you see whether a company is becoming more or less productive over time.

Grow Your Profits by Streamlining Your Business

by Jamie Bonomo and Andy Pasternak

Managers today are under intense pressure to deliver revenue growth. But as they and their teams respond to this challenge, they may unwittingly introduce complexity that drags down overall profitability. People in design, sales, and marketing, for example, are driven to introduce new products, acquire new customers, and enter new markets—and they often add offerings, channels, brands, and customers one at a time without regard to the cumulative impact on the business.

What is this cumulative impact? As a business becomes more complex, it gets difficult to trace costs to their origins. So senior managers struggle to figure out

---

Adapted from *Harvard Management Update* (product #U0505A), May 2005

which offerings and markets are profitable. They have a hard time deciding what to sell, at what price, and to whom. Digging into the costs of individual products, brands, channels, and customers helps managers at all levels in a company better understand each link in the value chain. That knowledge will help leaders as they refine strategy and others as they execute it.

Consider the following ways companies can simplify to increase profitability:

1. Analyze profitability by offering or market

Large, complex companies often lack consistent information and systems across their many businesses and geographies. Moreover, **shared costs**—those that cannot be directly attributed to individual offerings or markets—represent a large portion of their total cost structure. But you can determine true costs by digging into the details. Profitability analysis of this sort will typically reveal large profit disparities among lines of business, brands, products, and customers.

At a consumer products company we'll call Consolidated, Inc., for instance, managers viewed a longtime large account, MacGuffin, as one of its two most important customers in a particular region. However, the prices MacGuffin paid were low, and the complexity of serving the account was staggering, given the nearly 30 product stock-keeping units (SKUs) developed specifically for this customer. Consolidated used four manufacturing facilities to produce the SKUs and operated a "mixing center" to aggregate orders across plants, primarily for MacGuffin. Those costs had not been attributed to Mac-

Guffin but rather were spread across all accounts in the region. When managers analyzed the true cost of serving MacGuffin, from the sales front end to the operations back end, they realized the account *lowered* the bottom line by $700,000 even though it generated $5 million in annual sales. To lower costs and add value, Consolidated reduced MacGuffin's SKU count by 60%, repriced certain products, and restructured supply terms.

As this example shows, decisions about product selection and pricing should not be made on the margin—that is, you shouldn't assume that the cost of infrastructure is fixed and existing excess capacity is essentially free. While appealing in the short term, this approach may accommodate unprofitable offerings.

2. Make sure your brands and SKUs are pulling their weight

Most complex companies have many brands or SKUs that contribute little to the bottom line. A detailed analysis by one U.S. computer maker showed managers that many of its low-volume products had only modest customer reach, low revenues, and low profits—yet those offerings added considerable complexity to the manufacturer's operations. Indeed, the company had been using up to 20% of its assets to support these marginal brands and products. By targeting profitable brands and SKUs and cutting the rest loose, it freed up significant capacity with negligible loss of revenue and volume.

This was not a purely operations-driven effort, however. The company also incorporated customers' perspectives. Through rigorous research that blended survey and

QUESTIONS FOR MANAGERS

- Do you know which of your customers, brands, and product lines bring in profits? Do you know which ones lose money?
- If a new and highly profitable opportunity came along and your company did not have enough capacity to address it, what would it do?
- Do support functions such as R&D, sales, and marketing set their own agendas, or do they collaborate closely with other groups across the enterprise?
- Are performance metrics designed to optimize overall profitability?

testing tools from psychology and economics, the computer maker estimated demand for its various brands and SKUs and learned exactly how and why customers chose those products. With the data in hand, managers could evaluate which trade-offs in volume, pricing, and systemwide costs would help profitability.

3. Consolidate production

Another way to simplify is to improve the mix of low-cost and high-cost production capacity. Eliminating or cutting back on a single account to reduce indirect costs is just the first step. If a company streamlines a sufficiently large number of accounts, it can consolidate facilities and close the highest-cost production lines or service centers. The resulting efficiencies will give managers more leeway in negotiating pricing, and will help them end relationships with accounts that still perform poorly. This approach can dramatically boost profitability through operating-margin improvements and focus resources on accounts with high growth potential.

Transforming a revenue culture into a profit culture is no small task. All functions—from sales to marketing to operations—must join in the effort. But once your firm's processes and metrics are based on an integrated perspective, you'll be one step closer to a simpler and more profitable business.

Jamie Bonomo is a managing director, and **Andy Pasternak** is a director, of New York–based Mercer Management Consulting.

Working Your Assets to Boost Your Growth

by Miles Cook, Pratap Mukharji, Lorenz Kiefer, and Marco Petruzzi

Supply chains can account for a staggering 80% of an organization's costs. And at product companies, up to 60% of net assets go toward inventory, plants, warehouses, and other supply chain assets. Yet companies seldom look at supply chain improvements as a way to boost **return on invested capital**, or **ROIC.**

Calculating ROIC can be a little complex, but here's how it's usually done:

$$\frac{\text{Earnings + Interest Expense (with an Adjustment for the Tax Benefit of Interest Costs)}}{\text{Total Assets – Cash – Non-interest-bearing Current Liabilities}}$$

Adapted from *Harvard Management Update* (product #P0503B), March 2005

Companies most often focus on growing ROIC by building up the numerator: earnings. But shrinking the less-obvious denominator by accelerating asset turns—achieving the same or better results with fewer assets—can also have a huge impact. In our experience, introducing effective customer-centric supply chain management techniques can improve ROIC by an average of nearly 30%. And as a bonus, companies that trim down assets also significantly outgrow their competitors in revenue.

Embedding Supply Chain Math in Customer-Focused Decisions

Firms looking to boost ROIC can use supply chain economics to answer three key questions involving customers:

1. **What do we sell?** Can we streamline stock-keeping units (SKUs) and eliminate complexity, costs, and assets? For instance, perhaps we can cut some low-volume or unprofitable products and reduce the number of available options on others. That will make our plants more efficient and allow us to reduce inventory.

2. **To whom do we sell?** Do we have the right marketplace focus? In other words, are we aiming our supply chain capabilities where they can make money for the company? An analysis of profitability by customer, region, and channel may turn up some areas that are relatively (or even absolutely) unprofitable.

3. **How can we best deliver our offerings?** Are our infrastructure and service policies doing the job efficiently? We typically bundle our most complex products with an extended warranty and maintenance agreement. But is that the best deal for our customers—and does it help our bottom line?

Since their jobs begin and end with the customer, supply chain leaders are increasingly focusing on customer segmentation. A better understanding of what users want creates a better understanding of which products will satisfy them. Supply chain leaders can then establish different service levels for different customers and products. Dow Corning, for instance, had originally tried to differentiate its silicone-based products by bundling them with a lot of value-added services, such as technical support. But as Bain & Company consultants Mark Gottfredson and Steve Schaubert point out in their book *The Breakthrough Imperative* (Collins, 2008), some of Dow's customers didn't need these services and didn't want to pay for them. In response, Dow introduced a standard product line that could be ordered over the internet, without any application or engineering services included. It also began to offer its value-added services on an à la carte basis, so that customers could buy only what they needed.

Supply chain leaders typically vary their forecasting and demand planning for products depending on volumes, production requirements, and lead times. They're

IMPROVING GROWTH BY "FIXING THE DENOMINATOR"

A great example of a company that used supply chain improvements to boost growth is Groupe Danone, the French food conglomerate. During a turbulent period several years ago, it lost its leadership position in yogurt sales in Brazil. Nestlé had eclipsed Danone in market share, and Danone—also under attack by Parmalat—had stopped making money. The company needed to do something fast.

Conventional wisdom held that Danone couldn't match the two giants in operational efficiency, given their vast scale advantages. The two competitors also had wider distribution networks and more power within the trade. Danone initially concluded that the only way out was to compete on quality and innovation, not the easiest thing to do in a basic food category. Yet a streamlined supply chain saved the day.

Above all else, Danone's executives realized, people wanted fresher yogurt: They didn't like buying anything that was approaching its sell-by date. Indeed, when the company surveyed consumers, about half said they based their buying decisions on expiration dates.

To figure out how to give them exactly what they wanted, Danone answered the three key customer-focused questions driving supply chain math and concluded that it could improve how it got products into customers' hands. For one thing, volumes weren't always tied to demand: To reduce production costs, manufacturing had been told it could produce only full vats of yogurt for any SKU, which led to waste. For another, Danone uncovered problems in how its product moved from the factory to retail outlets. Inventory was scattered over multiple locations across the country, yet 80% of its yogurt sales took place within a half-day travel radius of its central warehouse—meaning that a large percentage of its product was making an unnecessary second stop in a regional facility. Such logistics resulted in less-than-fresh yogurt and stockouts where demand was high. Moreover, rigid maintenance and clean-up schedules added downtime that created more deviation between store-ordered volumes and the amount of yogurt actually produced.

So Danone's team redesigned its Brazilian distribution network to serve the majority of its store customers, turning three regional warehouses into transit points without inventory. It created new rules for production, allowing manufacturing to make partial vats of yogurt when needed. The company moved most of the supply chain responsibility under a centralized logistics organization that had more oversight over the forecasting process. The result? The average number of days from factory to store fell by more than half, to four.

(*continued*)

(continued)

By fixing the denominator on ROIC, Danone liberated its numerator. There was no change other than increased freshness, but consumers responded dramatically, increasing Danone's revenue by more than 10%, as well as boosting the company's return on sales.

also constantly weeding out inefficiencies rooted in silo-based thinking. In other words, they manage the link between supply chain decisions and manufacturing operations effectively, so that their companies concentrate on items that serve their target market with the least possible complexity. In the mid-1990s, for instance, the vehicle and engine maker Navistar introduced its Diamond Spec program, through which buyers of certain trucks could choose among 16 preengineered modules rather than the thousands of possible configurations that had been available. Soon thereafter, say Gottfredson and Schaubert, Diamond Spec "accounted for 80 percent of dealer orders for that class of truck"—and Navistar's costs were significantly lower.

How Goodyear's Customer Focus Improved Sales

Consider the supply chain situation at Goodyear Tire & Rubber Company several years ago. As a new chairman and chief executive took the reins, the company's North American Tire (NAT) operations were sliding toward a significant loss. Poorly targeted attempts to reduce inventories had led to declining service levels and frequent stockouts. Customers were complaining, and the company faced a clutter of obsolescent and unprofitable inventory in its warehouses. To raise the stakes even higher, Goodyear was preparing to launch two products it hoped would be blockbusters: its Assurance passenger-car tire and its redesigned commercial steer tire, aimed at curtailing Michelin's threat in the market for outfitting trucks.

How could Goodyear turn things around and strengthen sales? With a new president on board, NAT's management reexamined a full set of assumptions around "What do we sell?" and "To whom?" NAT created a team comprising sales, marketing, manufacturing, and finance that was given a broad charter for identifying and beginning to fix structural problems that ate up cash and working capital, and for starting to optimize customer service.

When the team took a clear-eyed look at what NAT sold and why, it saw, at the core of Goodyear's culture, a manufacturing-based mind-set focused chiefly on driving down unit costs, insufficiently balanced by considerations of downstream supply chain needs and customer requirements. The team cleaned house, reducing overall stocks 15% from seasonal highs and eliminating 50% of the company's unprofitable SKUs. And it reduced complexity: One streamlining initiative consolidated low-volume products from more than a dozen warehouses around the United States to one central place.

NAT also examined its service and delivery practices for product and customer segments. New guidelines allowed for expediting high-volume products (such as the company's Eagle performance tires) in lower quantities but stipulated batching low-volume, seasonal products (such as farm tires) and delivering them with longer lead times. Such practices started to align Goodyear's product profitability with the service requirements of different customer segments.

Improving supply chain performance demanded new discipline in sales forecasting. By sharing reliable data for demand planning in a joint sales and operations planning process, NAT developed a more realistic set of sales forecasts. NAT also fine-tuned its manufacturing schedule to parse monthly quotas to weeks and days required for given shipments, which reduced the need for safety stocks.

Such moves helped NAT "attack the denominator"—and as the changes took effect, customers noticed and appreciated improvements in the company's fill rates. Goodyear substantially reduced working capital tied up in inventory and freed up cash for other initiatives. As forecasting and other processes improved, the company reduced fluctuations in inventory, reducing peak-to-trough variance from 5.3 million units to 1.4 million just three years later. As it launched its new lines of tires, Goodyear balanced efforts to meet demand and control internal costs far better than it had in the past, even though the popularity of some tires required establishing dealer quotas based on their "fair share" of the market.

How did the supply chain math add up? After implementing the changes, Goodyear reported profits of

$36.5 million on sales of $4.7 billion, versus a net loss of $119.4 million on sales of $3.9 billion for the same period in the previous year. Better earnings combined with faster asset turns also boosted ROIC. The company attributed the financial improvements and profitable growth to better operating results in all business segments, including North American Tire.

Of course, applying supply chain science has organizational implications. Chief among these is the challenge of capturing the right statistics to accurately measure progress and eliminate hunch work. This also means tracking the performance metrics of vendors, logistics partners, and distributors—and sharing appropriate forecasts and other sensitive data. Few companies do these things well. Such focus has less to do with new IT systems than it does with people.

Companies should assign star players—and give them the proper incentives—to tackle the supply chain challenge. They should reward these executives not just for having enough stock on hand but also for increasing asset turns, growth, and share price.

Based in Atlanta, **Miles Cook** and **Pratap Mukharji** are Bain & Company partners who lead the firm's Global Supply Chain practice. **Lorenz Kiefer**, a partner in Düsseldorf, leads Bain's European Supply Chain practice. **Marco Petruzzi** is a partner based in Los Angeles.

Profit ≠ Cash (and You Need Both)

by Karen Berman and Joe Knight, with John Case

Profit, shown on the income statement, is not the same as **net cash,** shown on the cash flow statement. Why should this be? Some reasons are pretty obvious: Cash may be coming in from loans or from investors, and that isn't going to show up on the income statement at all. But even **operating cash flow** is not at all the same as **net profit.**

There are three essential reasons:

- **Revenue is booked at sale.** A sale is recorded whenever a company delivers a product or service. Ace Printing Company delivers $1,000 worth of brochures to a customer; Ace Printing Company re-

---

Adapted from *Financial Intelligence* (product #4989BC), by Karen Berman and Joe Knight, with John Case, Harvard Business Review Press, 2006

cords revenue of $1,000, and theoretically it could record a profit based on subtracting its costs and expenses from that revenue. But no cash has changed hands because Ace's customer typically has 30 days or more to pay. Since profit starts with revenue, it always reflects customers' promises to pay. Cash flow, by contrast, always reflects cash transactions.

- **Expenses are matched to revenue.** The purpose of the income statement is to tote up all the costs and expenses associated with generating revenue during a given time period. However, those expenses may not be the ones that were actually paid during that time period. Some may have been paid earlier. Some will be paid later, when vendors' bills come due. So the expenses on the income statement do not reflect cash going out. The cash flow statement, however, always measures cash in and out the door during a particular time period.

- **Capital expenditures don't count against profit.** A capital expenditure doesn't appear on the income statement when it occurs; only the depreciation is charged against revenue. So a company can buy trucks, machinery, computers, and so on, and the expense will appear on the income statement only gradually, over the useful life of each item. Cash, of course, is another story: All those items are often paid for long before they have been fully depreciated, and the cash used to pay for them will be reflected in the cash flow statement.

You may be thinking that in the long run cash flow will pretty much track net profit. Accounts receivable will be collected, so sales will turn into cash. Accounts payable will be paid, so expenses will more or less even out from one time period to the next. And capital expenditures will be depreciated, so over time the charges against revenue from depreciation will more or less equal the cash being spent on new assets. All this is true to a degree, at least for a mature, well-managed company. But the difference between profit and cash can create all sorts of mischief in the meantime, especially for a growing company. Entrepreneurial businesses in particular may face periods of fluctuating sales. They may have to cope with the fact that one big customer pays its bills very slowly—or that one important vendor requires payment up front. All these can wreak havoc on an entrepreneur's cash flow, even if they don't much affect profitability.

Profit Without Cash

We'll illustrate the difference between profit and cash by comparing two simple companies with dramatically different profit and cash positions. Sweet Dreams Bakery is a new cookies-and-cakes manufacturer that supplies specialty grocery stores. The founder has lined up orders based on her unique home-style recipes, and she's ready to launch on January 1. We'll assume she has $10,000 cash in the bank, and we'll also assume that in the first three months her sales are $20,000, $30,000, and $45,000. Cost of goods sold is 60% of sales, and her monthly operating expenses are $10,000.

Just by eyeballing those numbers, you can see she'll soon be making a profit. In fact, a simplified **income statement** for the first three months looks like this:

	January	**February**	**March**
Sales	$20,000	$30,000	$45,000
COGS	12,000	18,000	27,000
Gross profit	8,000	12,000	18,000
Expenses	10,000	10,000	10,000
Net profit	($ 2,000)	$ 2,000	$ 8,000

The **cash flow,** however, tells a different story. Sweet Dreams Bakery has an agreement with its vendors to pay for the ingredients and other supplies it buys in 30 days. But those specialty grocery stores that the company sells to? They're kind of precarious, and they take 60 days to pay their bills.

So here's what happens to Sweet Dreams' cash situation:

- In *January,* Sweet Dreams collects nothing from its customers. At the end of the month, all it has is $20,000 in receivables from its sales. Luckily, it does not have to pay anything out for the ingredients it uses, since its vendors expect to be paid in 30 days. (We'll assume that the COGS figure is all for ingredients, because the owner herself does all the baking.) But the company does have to pay expenses—rent, utilities, and so on. So all the initial $10,000 in cash goes out the door to pay expenses, and Sweet Dreams is left with no cash in the bank. A simplified representation of the company's checkbook would look like this:

Beginning cash	$10,000
Expenses	(10,000)
Ending cash	$ 0

- In *February,* Sweet Dreams still hasn't collected anything. (Remember, its customers pay in 60 days.) At the end of the month, it has $50,000 in receivables—January's $20,000 plus February's $30,000—but still no cash. Meanwhile, Sweet Dreams now has to pay for the ingredients and supplies for January ($12,000), and it has another month's worth of expenses ($10,000). So it's now in the hole by $22,000. Here's the checkbook (assuming for the moment that Sweet Dreams can show a negative balance in its bank account!):

Beginning cash	$ 0
Ingredients and supplies	(12,000)
Expenses	(10,000)
Ending cash	($22,000)

Can the owner turn this around? Surely, in March those rising profits will improve the cash picture! Alas, no.

- In *March,* Sweet Dreams finally collects on its January sales, so it has $20,000 in cash coming in the door, leaving it only $2,000 short against its end-of-February cash position. But now it has to pay for February's COGS of $18,000 plus March's expenses of $10,000. So at the end of March, it ends up $30,000 in the hole—a worse position than at the end of February. Again, the checkbook:

Beginning cash	($22,000)
Collections	20,000
Ingredients and supplies	(18,000)
Expenses	(10,000)
Ending cash	($30,000)

What's going on here? The answer is that Sweet Dreams is growing. Its sales increase every month, meaning that it must pay more each month for its ingredients. Eventually, its operating expenses will increase as well because the owner will have to hire more people. The other problem is the disparity between the fact that Sweet Dreams must pay its vendors in 30 days while waiting 60 days for receipts from its customers. In effect, it has to front the cash for 30 days—and *as long as sales are increasing, it will never be able to catch up unless it finds additional sources of cash.* As fictional and oversimplified as Sweet Dreams may be, this is precisely how profitable companies go out of business. It is one reason why so many small entrepreneurial companies fail in their first year. They simply run out of cash.

Cash Without Profit

But now let's look at another sort of profit/cash disparity.

Fine Cigar Shops is a start-up that sells very expensive cigars, and it's located in a part of town frequented by businesspeople and well-to-do tourists. Its sales for the first three months are $50,000, $75,000, and $95,000—

again, a healthy growth trend. Its cost of goods is 70% of sales, and its monthly operating expenses are $30,000 (high rent!). For the sake of comparison, we'll say that it, too, begins the period with $10,000 in the bank.

So Fine Cigar's **income statement** for these months looks like this:

	January	**February**	**March**
Sales	$50,000	$75,000	$95,000
COGS	35,000	52,500	66,500
Gross profit	15,000	22,500	28,500
Expenses	30,000	30,000	30,000
Net profit	($15,000)	($ 7,500)	($ 1,500)

Fine Cigar hasn't yet turned the corner on profitability, though it is losing less money each month. Meanwhile, what does its **cash** picture look like?

As a retailer, of course, Fine Cigar collects the money on each sale immediately. And we'll assume that it was able to negotiate good terms with its vendors, paying them in 60 days.

- In *January,* it begins with $10,000 and adds $50,000 in cash sales. It doesn't have to pay for cost of goods sold yet, so the only cash out the door is that $30,000 in expenses. End-of-the-month bank balance: $30,000. Here's a simplified representation of the company's checkbook:

Beginning cash	$10,000
Cash sales	50,000
Expenses	(30,000)
Ending cash	$30,000

- In *February,* Fine Cigar adds $75,000 in cash sales and still doesn't pay anything for cost of goods sold. So the month's net cash after the $30,000 in expenses is $45,000. Now the bank balance is $75,000! The checkbook:

Beginning cash	$30,000
Cash sales	75,000
Expenses	(30,000)
Ending cash	$75,000

- In *March,* Fine Cigar adds $95,000 in cash sales and pays for January's supplies ($35,000) and March's expenses ($30,000). Net cash in for the month is $30,000, and the bank balance is now $105,000. Here's the checkbook:

Beginning cash	$75,000
Cash sales	95,000
Payment of invoices	(35,000)
Expenses	(30,000)
Ending cash	$105,000

Cash-based businesses—retailers, restaurants, and so on—can thus get an equally skewed picture of their situation. In this case Fine Cigar's bank balance is climbing every month even though the company is unprofitable. That's fine for a while, and it will continue to be fine so long as the company holds down expenses so that it can turn the corner on profitability. But the owner has to be careful: If he's lulled into thinking that his business is doing great and that he can increase those expenses, he's liable to continue on the unprofitable path. If he fails to attain profitability, *eventually he will run out of cash.*

Fine Cigar, too, has its real-world parallels. Every cash-based business, from tiny Main Street shops to giants such as Amazon.com and Dell, has the luxury of taking the customer's money before it must pay for its costs and expenses. It enjoys the float—and if it is growing, that float will grow ever larger. But ultimately, the company must be profitable by the standards of the income statement; cash flow in the long run is no protection against unprofitability. In the cigar-store example, the losses on the books will eventually lead to negative cash flow; just as profits eventually lead to cash, losses eventually use up cash. It's the timing of those cash flows that we are trying to understand here.

Understanding the difference between profit and cash is a key to increasing your financial intelligence. It opens a whole new window of opportunity to make smart decisions. For example:

- **Finding the right kind of expertise.** The two situations described above require different skills. If a company is profitable but short on cash, then it needs financial expertise—someone capable of lining up additional financing. If a company has cash but is unprofitable, it needs operational expertise, someone capable of bringing down costs or generating additional revenue without adding costs. So financial statements tell you not only what is going on in the company but also what kind of expertise you need to hire.

- **Making good decisions about timing.** Informed decisions on when to take an action can increase a company's effectiveness. Take Setpoint Systems, a company that builds factory-automation systems, as an example. Managers at the company know that the first quarter of the year, when many orders come in, is the most profitable for the business. But cash is always tight because Setpoint must pay out cash to buy components and pay contractors. The next quarter, Setpoint's cash flow typically improves because receivables from the prior quarter are collected, but profits slow down. Setpoint managers have learned that it's better to buy capital equipment for the business in the second quarter rather than the first, even though the second quarter is traditionally less profitable, just because there's more cash available to pay for it.

The ultimate lesson here is that profit and cash are different—and a healthy business, both in its early years and as it matures, requires both.

Karen Berman and **Joe Knight** are the owners of the Los Angeles–based Business Literacy Institute. Coauthor **John Case** has written several popular books on management.

Why Cash Matters

by Karen Berman and Joe Knight, with John Case

There are three big reasons for understanding the **cash flow statement.**

First, it will help you see what is going on now, where the business is headed, and what senior management's priorities are likely to be. You need to know not just whether the overall cash position is healthy but specifically where the cash is coming from. Is much of it coming from regular business operations, rather than from lenders or investors? That's a good thing—it means the business itself is generating cash. Is investing cash flow a sizable negative number? If it isn't, that may mean the company isn't investing in its future. And what about financing cash flow? If investment money is coming in, that may be reason for optimism—or it may mean that

---

Adapted from *Financial Intelligence* (product #4986BC), by Karen Berman and Joe Knight, with John Case, Harvard Business Review Press, 2006

the company is desperately selling stock to stay afloat. Looking at the cash flow statement generates a lot of questions, but they are the right ones to be asking. Are we paying off loans? Why or why not? Are we buying equipment? The answers to those questions will reveal a lot about senior management's plans for the company.

Second, you *affect* cash. Most managers focus on profit when they should be focusing on both profit and cash. Of course, their impact is usually limited to operating cash flow—but that's one of the most important measures there is. For instance:

- **Accounts receivable.** Factors such as customers' satisfaction with your service, their relationship to your salespeople, and the accuracy of your invoices all help determine how customers feel about your company, and indirectly influence how fast they are likely to pay their bills. Disgruntled customers are not known for prompt payments—they like to wait until any dispute is resolved.

- **Inventory.** If you're in engineering, do you request special products all the time? If you do, you may be creating an inventory nightmare. If you're in operations and you like to have lots in stock, just in case, you may be creating a situation in which cash is just sitting on the shelves, when it could be used for something else.

- **Expenses.** Do you defer expenses when you can? Do you consider the timing of cash flow when making purchases? Obviously, we're not saying it's always wise to defer expenses; it's just wise to take into account what the cash impact will be when you do decide to spend money.

- **Giving credit.** Do you give credit to potential customers too easily? Alternatively, do you withhold credit when you should give it? Both decisions affect the company's cash flow and sales, which is why the credit department always has to strike a careful balance.

The list goes on. Maybe you're a plant manager, and you are always recommending buying more equipment, just in case the orders come in. Perhaps you're in IT, and you feel that the company always needs the latest upgrades to its computer systems. All these decisions affect cash flow, and senior management usually understands that very well. If you want to make an effective request, you need to familiarize yourself with the numbers that they're looking at.

Third, managers who understand cash flow tend to be given more responsibilities, and thus tend to advance more quickly, than those who focus purely on the income statement. You could go to someone in finance and say, "I notice our DSO [days sales outstanding] has been heading in the wrong direction over the last few months—how can I help turn that around?" Alternatively, you might learn the precepts of lean enterprise, which focuses on (among other things) keeping inventories to a minimum. A manager who leads a company in converting to lean thereby frees up huge quantities of cash.

Our general point here is that cash flow is a key indicator of a company's financial health, along with profitability and shareholders' equity. It's the final link in the triad.

Karen Berman and **Joe Knight** are the owners of the Los Angeles–based Business Literacy Institute. Coauthor **John Case** has written several popular books on management.

Your Balance Sheet Levers

by Karen Berman and Joe Knight, with John Case

Most companies use their cash to finance customers' purchase of products or services. That's the "accounts receivable" line on the balance sheet—the amount of money customers owe at a given point in time, based on the value of what they have purchased before that date.

The key ratio that measures accounts receivable is **days sales outstanding,** or **DSO**—that is, the average number of days it takes to collect on these receivables. *The longer a company's DSO, the more working capital is required to run the business.* Customers have more of its cash in the form of products or services not yet paid for, so that cash isn't available to buy inventory, deliver more

---

Adapted from *Financial Intelligence* (product #4977BC), by Karen Berman and Joe Knight, with John Case, Harvard Business Review Press, 2006

services, and so on. Conversely, the shorter a company's DSO, the less working capital is required to run the business. It follows that the more people understand DSO and work to bring it down, the more cash the company will have at its disposal.

Managing DSO

The first step in managing DSO is to understand what it is and in which direction it has been heading. If it's higher than it ought to be, and particularly if it's trending upward (which it nearly always seems to be), managers need to begin asking questions.

Operations and R&D managers, for example, must ask themselves whether there are any problems with the products that might make customers less willing to pay their bills. Is the company selling what customers want and expect? Is there a problem with delivery? Quality problems and late deliveries often provoke late payment, just because customers are not pleased with the products they're receiving and decide that they will take their own sweet time about payment. Managers in quality assurance, market research, product development, and so on thus have an effect on receivables, as do managers in production and shipping. In a service company, people who are out delivering the service need to ask themselves the same questions. If service customers aren't satisfied with what they're getting, they too will take their time about paying.

Customer-facing managers—those in sales and customer service—have to ask a similar set of questions. Are our customers financially healthy? What is the standard in their industry for paying bills? Are they in a region of the world that pays quickly or slowly? Salespeople typically have the first contact with a customer, so it is up to them to flag any concerns about the customer's financial health. Once the sale is made, customer-service reps need to pick up the ball and learn what's going on. What's happening at the customer's shop? Are they working overtime? Laying people off? Meanwhile, salespeople need to work with the folks in credit and customer service so that everybody understands the terms up front and will notice when a customer is late. At one company we worked with, the delivery people knew the most about customers' situations because they were at their facilities every day. They would alert sales and accounting if there seemed to be issues cropping up in a customer's business.

Credit managers need to ask whether the terms offered are good for the company and whether they fit the credit histories of the customers. They need to make judgments about whether the company is giving credit too easily or whether it is too tough in its credit policies. There's always a trade-off between increasing sales on the one hand and issuing credit to poorer credit risks on the other. Credit managers need to set the precise terms they're willing to offer. Is net 30 days satisfactory—or should we allow net 60? They need to determine strategies such as offering discounts for early pay. For example, "2/10 net 30" means that customers get a discount of 2% if they pay their bill in 10 days and no discount if they wait 30 days. Sometimes a 1% or 2% discount can help a struggling company collect its receivables and thereby lower its DSO—but of course it does so by eating into profitability.

We know of a small company that has a simple, homegrown approach to the issue of giving credit to customers. It has identified the traits it wants in its customers and has even named its ideal customer Bob. Bob's qualities include the following:

- He works for a large company.
- His company is known for paying its bills on time.
- He can maintain and understand the product provided (this company makes complex technology-intensive products).
- He is looking for an ongoing relationship.

If a new customer meets these criteria, he will get credit from this small manufacturer. Otherwise he won't. As a result of this policy, the company has been able to keep its DSO quite low and to grow without additional equity investment.

All these decisions can have a huge impact on accounts receivable and thus working capital. Reducing DSO even by one day can save a large company millions of dollars per day.

Managing Inventory

Many managers (and consultants!) these days are focusing on inventory. They work to reduce it wherever possible. They use buzzwords such as **lean manufacturing,**

just-in-time inventory management, and **economic order quantity (EOQ).** The reason for all this attention is exactly what we're talking about here. Managing inventory efficiently reduces working capital requirements by freeing up large amounts of cash.

The challenge is to reduce inventory to a minimum level while still ensuring that every raw material and every part will be available when needed and every product will be ready for sale when a customer wants it. A manufacturer needs to be constantly ordering raw material, making things, and holding them for delivery to customers. Wholesalers and retailers need to replenish their stocks regularly to avoid the dreaded stockout—an item that isn't available when a customer wants it. Yet every item in inventory can be regarded as frozen cash, which is to say cash that the company cannot use for other purposes. Exactly how much inventory is required to satisfy customers while minimizing that frozen cash? Well, that's the million-dollar question (and the reason for all those consultants).

Many different kinds of managers affect a company's use of inventory—which means that all these managers can help reduce working capital requirements. For example:

- **Salespeople** love to tell customers they can have exactly what they want. ("Have it *your* way," as the old Burger King jingle put it.) Custom paint job? No problem. Bells and whistles? No problem. But every variation requires a little more inventory, meaning a little more cash. Obviously, customers must be satisfied. But that commonsense requirement has to be balanced against the fact that inventory costs money. The more that salespeople can sell standard products with limited variations, the less inventory their company will have to carry.

- **Engineers** love those same bells and whistles. In fact, they're constantly working to improve the company's products, replacing version 2.54 with version 2.55 and so on. Again, this is a laudable business objective, but one that has to be balanced against inventory requirements. A proliferation of product versions puts a burden on inventory management. When a product line is kept simple with a few easily interchangeable options, inventory declines and inventory management becomes a less taxing task.

- **Production departments** greatly affect inventory. For instance, what's the percentage of machine downtime? Frequent breakdowns require the company to carry more work-in-process inventory and more finished-goods inventory. And what's the average time between changeovers? Decisions about how much to build of a particular part have an enormous impact on inventory requirements. Even the layout of a plant affects inventory: A well-designed production flow in an efficient plant minimizes the need for inventory.

Along these lines, it's worth noting that many U.S. plants eat up tremendous amounts of working capital.

When business is slow, they nevertheless keep on churning out product in order to maintain factory efficiency. Plant managers focus on keeping unit costs down, often because that goal has been pounded into their heads for so long that they no longer question it. They have been trained to do it, told to do it, and paid (with bonuses) for achieving it.

When business is good, that goal makes perfect sense: Keeping unit costs down is simply a way of managing all the costs of production in an efficient manner. (This is the old approach of focusing only on the income statement, which is fine as far as it goes.) When demand is slow, however, the plant manager must consider the company's cash as well as its unit costs. A plant that continues to turn out product in these circumstances is just creating more inventory that will take up space on a shelf. Coming to work and reading a book might be better than building product that is not ready to be sold.

Any large company can save millions of dollars in cash, and thereby reduce working capital requirements, just by making modest improvements in its inventory management.

Karen Berman and **Joe Knight** are the owners of the Los Angeles–based Business Literacy Institute. Coauthor **John Case** has written several popular books on management.

What's Your Working Capital Model? A Case Study

by John Mullins and Randy Komisar

Imagine a working capital model where your customers pay you before your product or service is even produced, not to mention delivered. A good idea, right? Consider the subscription-based periodical publishing industry. From the bare-bones *Kiplinger Letter* (a subscription-based personal finance newsletter) to the complex workings of the *New York Times,* companies in the periodicals industry historically have had negative working capital.

Why is this? Periodicals publishers—whether they publish newsletters, newspapers, or magazines—tend to

---

Excerpted from *Getting to Plan B: Breaking Through to a Better Business Model* (product #5371BC), by John Mullins and Randy Komisar, Harvard Business Review Press, 2009

have almost no inventory, just some paper and ink. As soon as they print the current edition, out it goes. On the other hand, subscription fees are collected long before the publication is printed and shipped. That's good news if you want to drive working capital down. For the publisher, the cash the subscriber pays up front is what accountants call a **liability** (unearned subscriptions or deferred revenues, as they are often called on publishers' financial statements), since the publisher now "owes" the upcoming issues to the subscriber. The result of all this: modest **current assets** (limited mostly to accounts receivable from advertising not yet paid), large **current liabilities** (the issues due for the rest of the year, for example), and negative **working capital.**

Dow Jones & Company (Dow Jones)—known best for its newspaper, the *Wall Street Journal,* and its stock market index, the Dow Jones Industrial Average—is a case in point for negative working capital. Its business was based on this working capital model for more than a century. Then along came the digital revolution. Was it time for Plan B?

Let's start at the beginning. Founded in New York City in 1882 by Charles Henry Dow, Edward Davis Jones, and Charles Milford Bergstresser, print media was Dow Jones's bread and butter. The company started off producing daily, handwritten news bulletins called *flimsies,* delivered by messengers to subscribers in the Wall Street area of Manhattan. In 1883 the company started publishing the *Customers' Afternoon Letter,* which six years later became the *Wall Street Journal.* The four-page *Journal* could be purchased for 2 cents a copy. Advertising was sold for 20 cents per line. In 1902, Clarence Barron, who was one of Dow Jones's first employees, purchased Dow, Jones & Company for $130,000. He added a weekly financial publication, *Barron's,* in 1921. Decades later, in the 1970s, Dow Jones diversified, purchasing a number of local newspapers, increasing its circulation and reach and lessening its reliance on the financial markets.

But in the late 1980s, with the advent of digital media like the now-ubiquitous Bloomberg terminals that have sprouted on nearly every desk in the financial world, the *Wall Street Journal* started losing subscribers. Circulation dropped from a high of 2.11 million in 1983 to 1.95 million by 1989. Profits deteriorated. The publishing world was changing, the Internet had arrived, and electronic publishing became Dow Jones's Plan B. But moving from print to digital was no trivial task. That it believed it could do so was a huge leap of faith.

Let's take stock of Dow Jones's working capital model at the end of its old-economy heyday, in 1992. These were the noncash elements of its working capital at that time:

- Current assets (other than cash) = 37 days
  - Inventory: 4 days
  - Accounts receivable: 33 days (subscribers pay in advance, but advertisers pay in arrears; this figure reflects the latter)
- Current liabilities = 109 days
  - Accounts payable: 70 days

  - Unearned subscriptions: 39 days (subscriptions paid for but not yet delivered)
- Net of these elements = –72 days

That's seventy-two days' worth of customer cash, or about 20 percent (72 days out of the 365-day year = 19.7 percent) of 1992's $1.8 billion in revenue, that Dow Jones could use for other things. It's like having $360 million of free money, just sitting there, ready to use to buy printing presses, pay wages, or to develop new businesses! By paying its suppliers (of newsprint among other things) in an average of seventy days and by collecting people's subscriptions for its publications and newswires up front, Dow Jones had the ability to literally use other people's money to pay its bills. But the game was changing. Would the working capital model that was central to any publisher's success have to change as well?

Dow Jones Goes Digital

By 1992 the company had already launched DowVision, a news service customized for Dow Jones's corporate customers. DowVision delivered published text from the *Wall Street Journal, New York Times, Financial Times, Washington Post,* and *Los Angeles Times,* together with a premier version of the Dow Jones newswires, directly to corporate desktops. Pleased with its early progress, in 1995 Dow Jones's leadership went public with its new strategy. "We're taking our editorial standards to the Web, where a glut of information often makes searching for the right piece of information time-consuming and fruitless." The company saw two distinct segments for its electronic services: individuals or small companies and large enterprises, both of which it wanted to serve. Dow Jones developed new online services for individuals and small businesses, allowing them to use credit cards to purchase subscriptions or to pay for downloads of specific packages of information such as articles. Large enterprises on the other hand were expected to sign annual contracts for electronic access to Dow Jones's information, paid in advance, of course. The company's leaders had not forgotten what had gotten it this far, paid subscriptions up front!

Soon there was an online electronic supplement to the *Wall Street Journal*'s Money & Investing section, known as the "*Wall Street Journal* Interactive Edition" (known later as *WSJ Online* at WSJ.com). This electronic newspaper subscription service allowed individual users to browse articles online. Both DowVision and The Publications Library, a news archive, were made available for Web users, primarily serving large enterprises as research tools, on a subscription basis.

From 1999 through 2006, Dow Jones quickened its digital pace, developing a joint venture with Reuters to create Factiva, a Web-based source of current and archived global news—subscriptions paid up front, of course. NewsPlus, a Web-formatted enhancement of Dow Jones's newswires, and Dow Jones Financial Information Services, which gave financial professionals additional Web access to electronic media, information, and directories, were added. MarketWatch.com, which provided online business and financial news, was acquired. Dow Jones's digital Plan B was well under way.

In 2006, Dow Jones went further, getting rid of some of its paper-based products in favor of online offerings. It launched *Barron's Online* and bought Factiva outright, terminating the joint venture with Reuters. In December it sold six of the community newspapers that it had published for years. CEO Rich Zannino said, "This sale and the pending acquisition of Factiva are the latest examples of our commitment to transform Dow Jones from a company heavily dependent on print publishing revenue to a more diversified company capable of meeting the needs of its customers across all consumer and enterprise media channels, whether print, online, mobile or otherwise."

Would Its Subscription-Reliant Working Capital Model Still Work?

The Dow Jones management team consisted of veterans who understood the crucial role that the working capital model played in the publishing industry. When they adopted Plan B and its new digital revenue model, they retained a crucial element of Plan A—the company's working capital model. Take a look at the 2006 Dow Jones numbers to see what happened:

- Current assets (other than cash) = 58 days
  - Inventory: 3 days
  - Accounts receivable: 55 days
- Current liabilities = 135 days

  - Accounts payable: 88 days
  - Unearned subscriptions: 47 days
- Net of these elements = –77 days

The Dow Jones's working capital model had improved to –77 days in 2006 (compared with –72 days in 1992)! The bedrock of the model, paid subscriptions up front, was still in place. The company still charged for traditional subscriptions for the *Wall Street Journal* and its remaining local newspapers, and for *Barron's,* Factiva, and its newswires. Most components of *Barron's Online* and WSJ.com required a subscription, as did some elements of MarketWatch. The Dow Jones indexes were both subscription- and license-based. And *Dow Jones Online News* could be licensed for a fee. Only a few experiments, such as CareerJournal.com, RealEstateJournal.com and OpinionJournal.com, came subscription-free.

The business had been transformed without going hat-in-hand to investors, funded largely by its customers' cash, and its precious working capital model had remained intact. The results for Dow Jones shareholders? Net income more than tripled on virtually the same $1.8 billion in revenue, rising from $107 million in 1992 to $386 million in 2006. And, perhaps with a nod to the company's successful transition to the digital age, Rupert Murdoch's News Corporation purchased Dow Jones for $5 billion in August 2007. Notably, and probably with thanks to Dow Jones's veterans, Murdoch, who indicated before the acquisition that he would make *WSJ Online* free and ad-based, has left its subscription-based, negative working capital model in place.

Lessons from Dow Jones

Dow Jones & Company shows us that negative working capital is helpful in coping with dramatic changes, such as those it faced in the digital revolution. Such a model provides customer cash with which to develop new products and strategies to iterate toward Plan B. Equally important was its management team's ability to identify new kinds and forms of content—new products, each of which was a leap of faith until proven—that consumers and business customers would value and pay for.

By itself, a better working capital model is not enough. Indeed, this point is evidenced by the cash infusion the *New York Times* needed in January 2009 from Carlos Slim, the Mexican billionaire, in order to remain afloat. The *Times* had not been nearly as inventive as Dow Jones in developing cash-generative digital offerings to make its own digital transition. While Dow Jones largely maintained its subscription-based model as it went digital, the *New York Times* did otherwise in making the *New York Times Online* free.

Dow Jones & Company also shows how a powerful working capital model, common to an entire industry in this case, can enable changes in other parts of one's strategy and make seemingly wrenching changes appear as smooth as silk. Though sailing was not always easy for Dow Jones—there were a couple of loss-making years along the way—its transition to the digital age was, for the most part, successful. Sometimes, though, it takes innovators to bring new and different working capital models to an established industry. When they do, watch out!

John Mullins is an associate professor of management practice at London Business School. **Randy Komisar** is a partner at Kleiner Perkins Caufield & Byers and a lecturer on entrepreneurship at Stanford University.

Learn to Speak the Language of ROI

by John O'Leary

Nobody is getting approval to spend money these days unless he or she can demonstrate an economic return. And so nonfinancial professionals are having to master the mysterious lexicon of **return on investment (ROI),** which includes terms such as **breakeven, internal rate of return,** and **discounted cash flow.**

These concepts should be second nature for anyone charged with making or contributing to financial decisions. But in too many companies, it's only the finance mavens who really understand ROI.

Say you want to spend $200,000 on a new automated call system. You're jazzed up about how reducing wait times from 60 seconds to 30 seconds will boost customer satisfaction and loyalty. As important as such improve-

Adapted from *Harvard Management Update* (product #U0210C), October 2002

ments are, they're not what the green-eyeshade types in finance care most about. For them, the key benefit is adding more money to the bottom line. Since they're the ones making the decision on your project, not only do you have to understand how the new system will increase profits, you must also be able to use the language of financial modeling to make the case for your initiative.

To get your project funded, especially when money is tight, here's what you need to learn.

Cash Flow Modeling

An ROI analysis enables you to compare the financial consequences of two (or more) business alternatives. Should we spend X dollars to do Project A or Y dollars to do Project B? Would we be better off buying or leasing? Would it be better to create this product in-house or to outsource?

To answer such questions you have to build a business case—a financial story based on facts, reasonable assumptions, and logic. At the heart of this story is a picture of the expected cash flow. A cash flow projection provides estimates of the net financial impact of a decision over a period of time. To construct such a projection, you must document not only all of the expected costs and benefits of the decision but also the time period in which they occur. Most ROI calculations seek to project three to five years out.

Here it's important to highlight a crucial difference between an ROI analysis and an income, or profit-and-loss (P&L), statement. The ROI analysis is cash-based, whereas a P&L uses standard accounting principles to spread out costs in a reasonable fashion. For example, on

BUILDING THE FINANCIAL CASE

The following ROI analysis makes projections for the launch of a fictitious new product, the RT-200. As with many cash flow analyses, this spreadsheet compares the financial consequences of investing in the launch of the RT-200 against the alternative of *not* launching the product (which carries no cost or return).

US$ in thousands	**Year 1**	**Year 2**	**Year 3**	**Year 4**	**Total**
Financial benefit (revenue or cost savings)					
Revenue	–	500	1,000	1,500	3,000
(Lost revenue)	(50)	(100)	(100)	(100)	(350)
Cost savings	–	100	120	130	350
Total benefit	(50)	500	1,020	1,530	3,000
Investments/capital expenditures:					
Hardware	600	–	100	–	700
Licenses	200	–	–	–	200
Development	500	–	–	100	600
Subtotal capital	1,300	–	100	100	1,500
Operating expenses:					
Headcount	25	25	25	25	100
Fabrication		55	90	155	300
Marketing		420	130	50	600
Subtotal operating	25	500	245	230	1,000
Total investments	1,325	500	345	330	2,500

Return on investment **Total return = $500**

	Year 1	**Year 2**	**Year 3**	**Year 4**	**Total**
Total cash flow	(1,375)	–	675	1,200	500
Discounted cash flow (Present value) Assumes 10% discount rate	(1,375)	–	557	902	84

(*continued*)

(*continued*)

The bottom-line ROI analysis on the RT-200 project:

- The project will cost $2.5 million in capital and operating expenses during the next four years but will generate $3 million in additional revenue and cost savings, for a four-year ROI of 20%.
- The project will be at breakeven during Year 4.
- The payback period for this investment is between three and four years.
- The net present value of this investment is $84,000, assuming a discount rate (or cost of capital) of 10%.
- The internal rate of return is 12.5%.

a P&L, an expenditure for a piece of equipment with a useful life of five years might be amortized on a straight-line basis over that time frame, with one-fifth of the cost hitting the P&L each year. On a cash flow statement, the charge hits in the time period that you send the check out the door.

Often an important element of building a cash flow is translating "soft" benefits into hard numbers. If you work for an airline and want to increase passenger legroom, it would be easy to calculate the hard costs of removing several rows of seats. But how would you quantify the benefits of having happier, more comfortable passengers?

One approach might be through survey data showing that, say, 10% of your passengers would be willing to pay a 15% premium for more legroom. And don't forget to estimate the financial impact of the higher customer retention you might experience because of your roomier seats, or of the new customers you might win over. You may want to build a spreadsheet to see how your estimate of the financial benefit changes as you alter your assumptions.

Once you've finished estimating all the positive and negative cash flows associated with the decision in question, summarize the cash flow by calculating the net impact for each time period. At that point, you're ready to start analyzing the results using the following methods of comparison:

- **Payback period.** This is the point at which all the costs expended have been recovered. Many companies have a benchmark of five to seven years as a maximum payback period.

- **Breakeven point.** This is the moment when costs are matched by increased revenue or cost savings for that period. The time between the breakeven point and the end of the payback period will vary according to how significantly revenues outpace costs after the breakeven point has been reached.

- **Discounted cash flow (DCF).** This is a summarized cash flow that accounts for the time value of money, which is an adjustment for the fact that

$100 received today is worth more than $20 a year for the next five years. The DCF shows the impact of your project in today's dollars. The present value of $100 in the future is calculated with the following formula:

$$\text{Present Value} = \$100 / (1+x)^n$$

where n is the number of years into the future that the benefit (or cost) will occur, and x is the interest rate expressed in hundredths.

- **Net present value (NPV).** The sum of all the present values in the discounted cash flow, the NPV gives you a sense of the absolute size of the return expected from a project. As shown in the example, the NPV of $84,000 means that the projected overall financial benefit of the project is equivalent to realizing an immediate gain of $84,000 (see "Building the Financial Case" on page 107). The NPV should be looked at in light of the size of the investment that will be made, which in this case is $2.5 million. Although any NPV above zero shows that doing the project is preferable to doing nothing, in practice the benchmark NPV to beat is not zero but how much the investment could have earned in an alternative project. (It's easy to calculate NPV on a business calculator or computer.)
- **Internal rate of return (IRR).** This is the interest rate at which the discounted cash flow yields a net present value of zero. This metric is of limited use, because it doesn't tell you how long you will enjoy

the given rate of return, nor does it show you the dollar amount of the return. Indeed, a pure IRR analysis can lead you to make poor decisions on competing investments.

Getting Your Budget Approved

Conducting the ROI analysis is just the first step. Now take it to the folks in finance. Don't bore them with talk about boosting customer satisfaction or reducing cycle times. Use the ROI analysis to spell out how your project will make the company money.

Let's return to the automated call system example: Your focus, when pitching this investment to the finance department, should be on how shorter wait times will mean fewer customers switching to competitors, which will translate into more revenue. Moreover, the new call system will require fewer customer service reps, which will also translate into lower costs.

This "dollars first" thinking will enable you to engage your audience in their passion—not yours. By describing your initiative in language that finance hears best, you're much more likely to win approval.

Boston-based business writer **John O'Leary** is the author of *Revolution at the Roots* (Free Press, 1995), a book about best practices in the public sector.

Practical Tools for Management Decisions

Finance and accounting provide a rich trove of practical tools that will help answer some of the most important management questions you'll ever face:

- What are the costs and benefits of a particular investment?
- What is its estimated return?
- How quickly will your company recoup the investment?
- How many units will it have to sell at specific prices to simply break even?
- Does your company have the right balance of fixed and variable costs?

Adapted from *Harvard Business Essentials: Finance for Managers* (product #5856BC), Harvard Business Review Press, 2002

- How can you estimate nonquantifiable costs and benefits?

Cost/Benefit Analysis

Suppose that Amalgamated Hat Rack is considering two investment options: (1) buying a new piece of machinery and (2) creating a new product line. The new machine is a smart-technology, high-temperature plastic extruder costing $100,000. Amalgamated believes that this machinery will save time and money over the long term and is safer than the current machinery. The second option, launching a line of coat racks, will require a $250,000 investment in plant, equipment, and design. How can Amalgamated decide whether either option makes economic sense? By doing a **cost/benefit analysis.** This means evaluating whether, over a given time frame, the benefits will outweigh the associated costs.

First, though, it's important to understand the cost of the status quo. You want to weigh the relative merits of each investment against the negative consequences, if any, of not making the investment at all.

Cost/benefit analysis involves the following steps:

1. **Identify the costs associated with the new business opportunity.** Consider this year's up-front costs plus those you anticipate in subsequent years.

2. **Identify the benefits of additional revenues the investment will bring.** These revenues could come from more customers or from increased purchases by existing customers. Be sure to factor

in associated new costs; ultimately, that means you'll be looking at profit.

3. **Identify the cost savings to be gained.** Some are straightforward; others are subtle and difficult to quantify. More efficient processing, for instance, could save you money because fewer people are required to do the same work, or because the process requires fewer steps, or because the time spent on each step decreases.

4. **Map out the timeline for expected costs and revenues.** When do you expect the costs to be incurred? In what increments? When do you expect to receive the benefits (additional revenues or cost savings)? In what increments?

5. **Evaluate the nonquantifiable benefits and costs.** There may be several, such as whether the investment strengthens a firm's position with distributors and whether it will add unnecessary product or process complexity to the firm's operations.

Once all that's done, you're ready to begin evaluating the investment opportunities by using one or more of the analytical tools below: accounting return on investment, payback period, or breakeven analysis.

Accounting Return on Investment

Return on investment (ROI)—or, to use the more technical term, **accounting return on investment**—is not always the best measure of an investment's success. But because many managers still use ROI, it pays to understand how they look at it. Accounting return on investment can take the form of cost savings, incremental profit, or value appreciation. Let's look at the simplest possible way of figuring it, although as we'll see in a moment, it isn't very realistic. You would begin by determining the net return, simply by subtracting the total cost of the investment from the total benefits received. Then, to calculate the ROI, you would divide the return by the total cost of the investment.

Suppose the new $100,000 extruder Amalgamated is considering would realize an annual $18,000 in savings for the company over the lifetime of the machine, which is estimated to be seven years. The total savings would thus be $126,000 ($18,000 × 7), making for a net return of $26,000 ($126,000 – $100,000). If you divide the net return ($26,000) by the total cost of the investment ($100,000), you get an ROI of 26%.

But that isn't the true return on investment, because it ignores the time value of money. For example, which would you rather have (assuming equal risks): an investment that gave you a 26% return in one year, or one that gave you the same return at the end of seven years? No contest there. Any rational investor would want the money sooner rather than later. Thus, true ROI calculations must always factor in the time value of money. Depending on your assumptions, you might find that the true ROI on the extruder was 5% or 10% rather than 26%.

Would any of those percentages even be a good return on the investment? In isolation, such figures have no particular meaning, since ROI calculations are a way of comparing returns on money a company invests internally with returns available to it elsewhere at the *same level of risk*. The notion of equal risk is very important here. All investors demand higher returns for higher risk. It makes no sense to compare the returns the company believes it could make from an investment in A, the relatively safe expansion of a current product line, with an investment in B, a wholly new product line for an untested market. The risk levels of the two potential investments are simply not equivalent. The higher-risk investment should have a higher potential return.

Payback Period

Companies also want to know the **payback period:** how long it will take a particular investment to pay for itself. We already know that the plastic extruder is expected to save Amalgamated $18,000 a year. To determine the payback period, divide the total amount of the investment by the annual savings expected. In this case, $100,000 divided by $18,000 equals 5.56. In other words, the extruder will pay for itself in about five-and-a-half years.

What if we assume that the extruder will wear out after four years rather than five? The investment now appears to be not particularly attractive—certainly less attractive than an investment with a similar ROI and a payback period of three years. As an analytical tool, the payback period tells you only one thing: how long it will take to recoup your investment. Although it is not useful in comparing real alternatives, some executives still rely on it.

Breakeven Analysis

Breakeven analysis tells you how much (or how much more) you need to sell in order to pay for the fixed investment—in other words, at what point you will break even on your cash flow. With that information in hand, you can look at market demand and competitors' market shares to determine whether it's realistic to expect to sell that much. Breakeven analysis can also help you think through the impact of changing price and volume relationships.

Most companies do breakeven analysis on the basis of revenue and gross profit margin. Here we will take a simplified approach and do the figuring on the basis of unit volume, so you can see the underlying reality. Our breakeven calculation will help you determine the volume level at which the total after-tax contribution from a product line or an investment covers its total fixed costs.

Before you can perform the calculation, you need to understand the components that go into it:

- **Fixed costs.** These are costs that stay mostly the same, no matter how many units of a product or service are sold—costs such as insurance, management salaries, and rent or lease payments. For example, the rent on the production facility will be the same, whether the company makes 10,000 or 20,000 units, and so will the insurance.

- **Variable costs.** Variable costs are those that change with the number of units produced and sold. Examples include labor and the costs of raw materials. The more units you make, the more you consume these items.

- **Contribution margin.** This is the amount of money that every sold unit contributes to paying for fixed costs. It is defined as net unit revenue minus variable (or direct) costs per unit.

With these concepts understood, we can do the calculation with this straightforward equation:

Breakeven Volume = Fixed Costs / Unit Contribution Margin

First, find the unit contribution margin by subtracting the variable costs per unit from the net revenue per unit. Then divide total fixed costs, or the amount of the investment, by the unit contribution margin. The quotient is the breakeven volume—that is, the number of units that must be sold for all fixed costs to be covered.

To see breakeven analysis in practice, let's look again at the plastic extruder example. Suppose that each hat rack produced by the extruder sells for $75, and that the variable cost per unit is $22:

$75 (Price per Unit) – $22 (Variable Cost per Unit) = $53 (Unit Contribution Margin)

Therefore:

$100,000 (Total Investment Required) / $53 (Unit Contribution Margin) = 1,887 Units

In other words, Amalgamated must sell 1,887 hat racks to recover its $100,000 investment. At this point,

A BREAKEVEN COMPLICATION

Our Hat Rack breakeven analysis represents a simple case. It assumes that costs are distinctly fixed or variable and that costs and unit contributions will not change if output increases or decreases. These assumptions may not hold in the real world. Rent may be fixed up to a certain level of production and then increase by 50% as you rent a secondary facility to handle expanded output. Labor costs may in reality be a hybrid of fixed and variable. And as you push more and more of your product into the market, you may find it necessary to offer price discounts—which reduce contribution per unit. You will need to adjust the breakeven calculation to accommodate these untidy realities.

the company must decide whether the breakeven volume is achievable: Is it realistic to expect to sell 1,887 additional hat racks, and if so, how quickly?

Operating Leverage

Your goal, of course, is not to break even but to make a profit. Once you've covered all your fixed costs with the contributions of many unit sales, every subsequent sale contributes directly to profits. To restate the equation used earlier in slightly different form:

$$\text{Unit Net Revenue} - \text{Unit Variable Cost} = \text{Unit Contribution to Profit}$$

You can see at a glance that the lower the unit variable cost, the greater the contribution to profits will be. In the pharmaceutical business, for example, the unit cost of producing and packaging a bottle of a new wonder drug may be a dollar or less. Yet if the company can sell each bottle for $100, it captures $99 per bottle in profit once sales have exceeded the breakeven point! Of course, the pharmaceutical company may have invested $400 million up front in fixed product development costs just to get the first bottle out the door. It will have to sell many bottles just to break even. But if it can, the profits will be extraordinary.

The relationship between fixed and variable costs is often described in terms of **operating leverage**. Companies with high fixed costs and low variable costs have high operating leverage. This is true of businesses in the software industry, for instance, where fixed product-development outlays are the bulk of a firm's costs and the variable cost of the discs on which programs are distributed represent only pennies. By contrast, companies with low operating leverage have low fixed costs relative to the total cost of producing every unit of output. A law firm, for example, has a minimal investment in equipment and fixed expenses. Most of its costs are the fees it pays its attorneys, which vary depending on the hours they bill to clients.

Operating leverage is a great thing once a company passes its breakeven point, but it can cause substantial losses if breakeven is never achieved. In other words, it's risky. This is why managers give so much thought to finding the right balance between fixed and variable costs.

Amalgamated Hat Rack, Coat Rack Division, January budget-to-actual

	Budget Jan.	Actual Jan.	Variance
Coat rack revenues	$39,000	$38,725	($275)*
Cost of goods sold	19,500	19,200	300
Gross margin	19,500	19,525	25
Marketing expense	8,500	10,100	(1,600)
Administrative expense	4,750	4,320	430
Total operating expense	13,250	14,420	(1,170)
Operating profit (EBIT)	$6,250	$5,105	($1,145)

*All parentheses indicate unfavorable variances.
Source: HMM Finance

Estimating Nonquantifiable Benefits and Costs

Because the numbers seldom tell the whole story, you'll need to look at qualitative factors too. For instance, how well does a potential investment fit the company's strategy and mission? Can the firm take it on without losing focus? How likely is it to succeed, given market conditions?

Even though such factors are not fully quantifiable, try to quantify them as much as possible. Say you're assessing the value of improved data—more comprehensive information that is easier to understand and more widely available—that a new investment would bring. You could try to come up with a dollar figure that represents the value of employees' time saved by the data, or the value of the increased customer retention that might be gleaned from your better understanding of purchase patterns. Such estimates should not necessarily be incorporated into your ROI or other quantified analyses, but they can be very persuasive nevertheless.

Weigh the quantifiable and the nonquantifiable factors together. For example, if an investment opportunity is only marginally positive according to the numbers, you may want to give equal weight to qualitative considerations (such as its likelihood to increase customer loyalty) in your final decision.

Tracking Performance

Once you've decided to undertake an investment opportunity, you should monitor its progress. Track your projections against actual revenues and expenses. It's a good idea to do this on a monthly basis, so that you can spot potential problems early on. With that in mind, let's look at projections for a new coat rack division at Amalgamated Hat Rack. The table on the previous page shows the state of affairs early in the first quarter.

The division is doing reasonably well on revenues and cost of goods sold. Its only really large negative variance is in the marketing expense line. Because the numbers are based on just the first month's figures, it is difficult to know if that variance is simply a onetime, or seasonal, variation, or if Amalgamated will have to spend more on marketing than anticipated. If your investment is not tracking according to budget, and if it looks as if the pattern of unexpectedly high costs (or unexpectedly low revenues) will hold, you may need to rethink the initiative—or even discontinue it.

Section 3
The Limits of Financial Data

This part of the *HBR Guide to Finance Basics for Managers* is a little different from the rest. In the earlier sections you learned the fundamentals. In this one you'll get some advice about how to evaluate what you know, how to use it most effectively, and how to supplement it with other kinds of information.

Why are such cautions necessary? Mainly because we tend to put too much faith in numbers. The income statement and balance sheet may seem precise, but they aren't. They reflect all sorts of assumptions, estimates, and procedural decisions, such as which depreciation method to use. Moreover, there is much about a business that the numbers—even the truly precise ones on the cash flow statement—can't capture. So when you use the financial statements, you have to exercise good judgment about what they're telling you and determine how they may be misleading you. The articles in this section will help.

What the Financial Statements Don't Tell You

by John Case

In 2006, one of the largest firms on Wall Street turned in perhaps its best performance ever. Earnings set a record for the fourth year in a row; pretax profit margin was a whopping 30.1%. "After several years of restructuring and investing in our business, all of the components came together to reflect a company capable of strong disciplined performance with tremendous potential for future success," wrote the chairman in his letter to shareholders.

The firm was Merrill Lynch. The following year it lost $8.6 billion—"the worst performance in the history of Merrill Lynch," as the (new) chairman acknowledged. In 2008 Bank of America agreed to buy Merrill in a distress sale, and in 2009 the firm ceased to exist as an independent entity.

. . .

In 2010, the chief executive of a major oil company reported a good deal of satisfaction with his company's financial results the previous year. Despite a harsh economic climate and a lower price for petroleum, return on sales had dropped only a fraction of a percentage point, and the company actually increased its dividend to shareholders by 2%. "A revitalized [company] kept up its momentum and delivered strong operating and financial results while continuing to focus on safe and reliable operations," he wrote to his shareholders on February 26.

The oil company was BP. Less than two months later, the drilling rig Deepwater Horizon *blew up, killing 11 people and unleashing the biggest offshore oil spill in history. The ultimate cost to BP—in money, in reputation, in its ability to operate around the world—wouldn't be known for years. BP's own estimates of direct costs came to roughly $40 billion.*

Grim stories such as these are cautionary tales about what you can and cannot discern just by scrutinizing a company's financials. It's true that finance is the language of business, and unless you can grasp it, you will be at a perpetual disadvantage in any kind of business career. But make no mistake: The financials describe only a fraction of a company's reality, and sometimes a misleading fraction at that.

So in this chapter we'll look not at what the financials tell you but at what they *don't* tell you. The figures themselves may be wrong or deceptive. They may be silent about a host of organizational matters that affect a company's success. They may capture a business reality that is true for the moment but that is about to be transformed by external events. Wise managers always keep one eye on the financial reports, the ultimate gauge of their performance. But they keep an equally sharp eye on all the nonfinancial or external factors that show up late, murkily, or not at all in the financial data. As we'll see, such factors fill in the rest of the picture.

Financial Sleight of Hand

One limitation of financial statements is that they can be manipulated. The usual goal, of course, is to make things look better than they really are.

The manipulation may take the form of outright fraud. The Italian company Parmalat—a multibillion-dollar food giant with operations in dozens of countries—defaulted on a bond payment in November 2003. Alarmed, auditors and lenders began scrutinizing the company's books, which seemed to show that Parmalat held nearly $5 billion in an account with Bank of America. In December, however, Bank of America reported that there was no such account. Parmalat wound up in bankruptcy, and some of its executives received prison sentences for the deception.

More often, the manipulation is subtler: A company simply alters its accounting practices. Accountants have a good deal of discretion over many items on the income statement and the balance sheet, and are free to adopt different procedures and assumptions as long as they deem the changes reasonable and apply them consistently. A company can change the way it values inventory, for example, or the amount that it sets aside for bad debt. Either move will trigger an adjustment—positive or negative—to the income statement and make the bottom line look better or worse. A company can also alter its depreciation schedule. If it owns a fleet of trucks or airplanes and decides that each one should last 12 years rather than 10, it will then record less depreciation on its income statement. Presto: The bottom line suddenly grows by a corresponding amount. In theory, any new procedure or assumption that is material to the company's results should appear in the footnotes to the financials. But the accountants get to decide whether the new way of doing things is material.

The line between fraud and a reasonable change in procedures isn't always clear. One telecommunications company got itself in trouble by taking a group of expenses that everyone else in the industry classified as operating expenses and inappropriately categorizing them as capital expenditures. Since only a part of a capital expenditure—depreciation—shows up on the income statement, the company's profits improved significantly. Some people in the company presumably believed that the change was justified. The Justice Department disagreed, characterizing the move as an "accounting trick" and issuing an indictment.

The moral here is that it pays to understand the assumptions and procedures used to calculate the financials. The statements themselves don't always tell the truth, the whole truth, and nothing but the truth.

Only One Piece of the Financial Puzzle

The three statements reveal a good deal, but not everything, about a company's financial position. For instance,

assets such as land, buildings, and equipment are recorded at historical cost on the balance sheet and depreciated accordingly—but nowhere does the balance sheet say what they might be worth on the open market today. (The continuing debate over "mark to market" accounting, in which companies use real or estimated market prices to value their assets, applies only to financial assets.) Merrill Lynch held plenty of assets, such as mortgage-backed securities. But when the housing bubble collapsed, those assets turned out to be worth far less than anybody had imagined.

Probably the most important financial fact the three major statements don't tell you is what a company as a whole is worth. The owners' equity line on the balance sheet, which you might think indicates value, really has nothing to do with what a buyer would have to pay to acquire the firm.

For publicly traded companies, the value of the entire enterprise is known as its **market capitalization,** or just **market cap.** This is the amount, in theory, that an investor would have to pay to buy all the shares of stock. To calculate market cap, you simply multiply the stock price by the total number of shares. The value changes daily, just because share prices move up and down. The price movements depend only partly on the performance reflected in financial statements. They also depend on what is happening to the market in general—that is, how interested investors are in buying stocks. General Electric's shares hit about 60 during the height of the dot-com boom in the early 2000s and plunged to about 6 during the depths of the financial crisis later in the decade. The company was performing somewhat differently during the two periods, but the gap in performance was nowhere near as great as the difference in share price and hence market cap.

Of course, it is rare for anyone to buy a publicly traded company at a figure close to its market cap on any given day. If an investor or potential acquirer announces an intention to scoop up all of a company's shares, the shares naturally rise in value. That's why prospective buyers typically have to pay a premium over the shares' value on the day of the announcement.

The value of a private company is harder to determine. A high-tech firm might be worth considerably more than its **book value,** or **owners' equity,** because a buyer would be hoping to acquire intangibles, such as engineering expertise or intellectual property. Neither of these asset categories shows up on the balance sheet. A small service company such as a marketing firm or a plumbing contractor, by contrast, might be worth considerably less than owners' equity would suggest. Its tangible assets—computers, telephone equipment, vehicles, inventory—may not yet be fully depreciated, but they may also have little value on the open market. For this kind of company, the real value lies in the experience, expertise, and contacts of the business owner. The buyer's motivations matter, too. An acquirer simply buying the business for its hard assets is likely to pay less than someone who wants to keep the enterprise as a going concern. A so-called strategic buyer—an acquirer that needs the private company to fill out its business lines, its technologies, or its geographic reach—may pay most of all.

Reaching Beyond the Financials

The financial statements are essentially backward-looking. The **income statement** and **cash flow statement** tell you how an organization performed along certain dimensions in a previous time period. The **balance sheet** gives you a snapshot of its financial health as of a given date. But a business also needs to know what is going on right now and what's likely to happen tomorrow. If its managers can do something about those factors in the present, they'll greatly improve their chances of seeing better results next quarter or next year.

Here are three key categories of information that you won't learn about from the financials:

1. The organization's nonfinancial health.

The explosion of the *Deepwater Horizon* in the Gulf of Mexico wasn't BP's first major accident in recent years. An explosion at the company's Texas City refinery in 2005 killed 15 people and injured 180 more. Later that year another BP drilling platform in the Gulf nearly sank because workers hurrying to finish it had installed a valve incorrectly. In 2006 BP's pipelines from Alaska's Prudhoe Bay field began to leak, eventually spilling 267,000 gallons—the area's worst spill ever. Somehow the company seemed unable to fix its recurrent safety problems. In 2009, reported *Fortune* magazine,

> *. . . the federal Occupational Safety and Health Administration (OSHA) proposed a record fine against BP for "failure to abate" previously cited hazards at Texas*

City. OSHA also cited BP for hundreds of new "willful" safety violations. (BP totaled 829 such refinery violations from June 2007 to February 2010, according to the Center for Public Integrity. The rest of the industry combined had 33.) There had been three more deaths at Texas City since the 2005 explosion.

If a company has safety issues like these, it's probably an unhealthy organization—that is, it's likely to experience one problem after another, regardless of what the financials might say about its *fiscal* health.

Safety is just one aspect of organizational health (and one that is far more relevant in mining or manufacturing than, say, in banking). Another is the level of employee engagement. Do people enjoy working at your company? Would they recommend it to a friend? To answer these questions you need data from employee surveys, for example, and from human-resources indicators such as employee retention rates. You won't find any of this information on the financials.

Healthy organizations are also nimble: Their people can make and execute good decisions without undue time or trouble. Bain & Company consultants Marcia Blenko, Paul Rogers, and Michael Mankins, in their book *Decide & Deliver* (Harvard Business Review Press, 2010), tell the story of ABB, the big Switzerland-based power equipment and automation company. ABB was much heralded in the 1990s for its radically decentralized structure, and for a while its financial performance lived up to the accolades. But a particular kind of rot was eating away at ABB from the inside: People were fighting tooth and nail over basic business decisions such as bidding on big power projects. "Overall, the company was structured into a complex labyrinth, with thousands of units operating on their own," the authors write. "Many of these local entities controlled factories and thus did all they could to sell the products those factories made, even if that meant discouraging customers from patronizing other ABB units." In effect, the company was hamstrung by its own structure. "With so many decisions requiring intense negotiations, internal politics grew bitter."

There is no direct information about organizational decisiveness in the financials. Many companies gather data about it through employee surveys, interviews, and internal focus groups. As with employee engagement, the results help executives understand why and how the company's future financial performance might suffer.

2. *What customers are thinking.*

Customer attitudes—their satisfaction with a company and its products, their gripes and complaints, their intent to repurchase, and so forth—also don't appear on the financials. Yet those attitudes are critical indicators of a company's future success. After all, if a firm can't hold on to its customers and attract new ones, its prospects are likely to be dim.

Determining customer attitudes requires several different kinds of research. The periodic customer-satisfaction surveys that most large companies conduct provide a starting point. (The quality of this data is often suspect, however. For instance, a company may encourage its customers to give it high marks when the surveyor calls, as many auto dealerships do.) It is probably more helpful to scrutinize customer behavior. How long do your customers stay with you? What percentage of them buy only once and then are never heard from again? What is your "share of wallet"—that is, how much of their total spending in your categories do you get? Many companies also make a point of creating communities of customers to advise them on policies, new products, and the like. LEGO encourages and supports local hobbyists' clubs and conferences, and often creates new product kits based on ideas from the avid users who participate in such get-togethers.

3. *What competitors are planning.*

Every business is vulnerable to competitors, so the more you know about your rivals, the better off you are. This point is hardly original, and most companies spend a good deal of time and resources trying to anticipate competitors' next moves. Even so, they often are bested by rivals. Consider the following pitfalls:

- ***Ignoring the blind side.*** In the 1970s and 1980s, General Motors, Ford, and Chrysler competed fiercely with one another—and famously failed to notice the onslaught of lower-cost, higher-quality vehicles being imported from Japan. It took years for Detroit's Big Three to catch up with Toyota, Nissan, and Honda in cost and quality. Meanwhile the U.S. companies lost huge amounts of market share to the imports.

- ***Ignoring upstarts.*** Xerox once dominated the market for photocopiers. When Canon came along with a small, inexpensive, slow-operating copier designed for small businesses and home offices, Xerox didn't pay much attention. As Harvard Business School professor Clayton M. Christensen points out in his work on disruptive innovation, that made perfect sense—Xerox's customers weren't interested in cheap, underperforming machines. But Canon got a toehold in the market, and it was soon able to improve its machines, move up-market, and challenge Xerox head-on.

- ***Missing the next big thing.*** Nokia, once the leader among cell phone manufacturers, found itself upstaged and outcompeted by Apple's iPhone and other smart phones. Although it had introduced a smart phone of its own, it missed the appeal of touch-screen technology. So rapid was the company's fall that by 2010 Nokia was in danger of becoming a second-tier player, particularly in the United States.

Competitors' plans don't show up in any survey. Smart companies keep a careful eye on those plans by analyzing their competitors' reports and press releases, talking to knowledgeable analysts and observers, and attending industry conferences. A business that pays little attention to the competition does so at its peril.

It makes sense for every manager to read, understand, and stay on top of the financials—not just the three key statements, which are summaries, but day-to-day data on revenues, operating costs, performance to budget, and the like. But if you put too much trust in the numbers and fail to consider factors they don't capture, you're likely to wind up in trouble. To avoid the well-chronicled missteps of Merrill Lynch, BP, and others, search *everywhere* for the information you need, and make sure you get it in a timely, useful fashion. If you wait to see the last period's financials, it will be too late.

John Case is a consulting writer to a variety of clients, including Bain & Company and the Business Literacy Institute. He is the author or coauthor of more than a dozen books on business and management.

The Five Traps of Performance Measurement

by Andrew Likierman

In an episode of *Frasier*, the television sitcom that follows the fortunes of a Seattle-based psychoanalyst, the eponymous hero's brother gloomily summarizes a task ahead: "Difficult and boring—my favorite combination." If this is your reaction to the challenge of improving the measurement of your organization's performance, you are not alone. In my experience, most senior executives find it an onerous if not threatening task. Thus they leave it to people who may not be natural judges of performance but are fluent in the language of spreadsheets. The inevitable result is a mass of numbers and comparisons that provide little insight into a company's performance and may

Reprinted from *Harvard Business Review*, October 2009 (product #R0910L)

even lead to decisions that hurt it. That's a big problem in the current recession, because the margin for error is virtually nonexistent.

So how should executives take ownership of performance assessment? They need to find measures, qualitative as well as quantitative, that look past this year's budget and previous results to determine how the company will fare against its competitors in the future. They need to move beyond a few simple, easy-to-game metrics and embrace an array of more sophisticated ones. And they need to keep people on their toes and make sure that today's measures are not about yesterday's business model.

In the following pages I present what I've found to be the five most common traps in measuring performance and illustrate how some organizations have managed to avoid them. My prescriptions aren't exhaustive, but they'll provide a good start. In any event, they can help you steal a march on rivals who are caught in the same old traps.

Trap 1: Measuring Against Yourself

The papers for the next regular performance assessment are on your desk, their thicket of numbers awaiting you. What are those numbers? Most likely, comparisons of current results with a plan or a budget. If that's the case, you're at grave risk of falling into the first trap of performance measurement: looking only at your own company. You may be doing better than the plan, but are you beating the competition? And what if the estimates you're seeing were manipulated?

To measure how well you're doing, you need information about the benchmarks that matter most—the ones outside the organization. They will help you define competitive priorities and connect executive compensation to relative rather than absolute performance—meaning you'll reward senior executives for doing better than everyone else.

The trouble is that comparisons with your competitors can't easily be made in real time—which is precisely why so many companies fall back on measurements against the previous year's plans and budgets. You have to be creative about how you find the relevant data or some proxy for them.

One way is to ask your customers. Enterprise, the car-rental company, uses the Enterprise Service Quality Index, which measures customers' repeat purchase intentions. Each branch of the company telephones a random sample of customers and asks whether they will use Enterprise again. When the index goes up, the company is gaining market share; when it falls, customers are taking their business elsewhere. The branches post results within two weeks, put them next to profitability numbers on monthly financial statements, and factor them into criteria for promotion (thus aligning sales goals and incentives).

Of course you have to make sure you don't annoy your customers as you gather data. Think about how restaurant managers seek feedback about the quality of their service: Most often they interrupt diners' conversations to ask if everything is OK; sometimes they deliver a questionnaire with the bill. Either approach can be irritating. Danny Meyer, the founder of New York's Union Square Hospitality Group, gets the information unobtrusively, through simple observation. If people dining together in one of his restaurants are looking at one another, the service is probably working. If they're all looking around the room, they may be wowed by the architecture, but it's far more likely that the service is slow.

Another way to get data is to go to professionals outside your company. When Marc Effron, the vice president of talent management for Avon Products, was trying to determine whether his company was doing a good job of finding and developing managers, he came up with the idea of creating a network of talent management professionals. Started in 2007, the New Talent Management Network has more than 1,200 members, for whom it conducts original research and provides a library of resources and best practices.

Trap 2: Looking Backward

Along with budget figures, your performance assessment package almost certainly includes comparisons between this year and last. If so, watch out for the second trap, which is to focus on the past. Beating last year's numbers is not the point; a performance measurement system needs to tell you whether the decisions you're making now are going to help you in the coming months.

Look for measures that lead rather than lag the profits in your business. The U.S. health insurer Humana, recognizing that its most expensive patients are the really sick ones (a few years back the company found that the sickest 10% accounted for 80% of its costs), offers customers incentives for early screening. If it can get more customers into early or even preemptive treatment than other companies can, it will outperform rivals in the future.

The quality of managerial decision making is another leading indicator of success. Boards must assess top executives' wisdom and willingness to listen. Qualitative, subjective judgments based on independent directors' own experience with an executive are usually more revealing than a formal analysis of the executive's track record (an unreliable predictor of success, especially for a CEO) or his or her division's financial performance. (See "Evaluating the CEO," by Stephen P. Kaufman, HBR October 2008.)

It may sound trite, but how the company presents itself in official communications often signals the management style of top executives. In August 2006 the *Economist* reported that Arijit Chatterjee and Donald Hambrick, of Pennsylvania State University, had devised a narcissism index on which to rate 105 company bosses, based on the prominence of the CEO's photo in the annual report, his or her prominence in press releases, the frequency of the first person singular in interviews with the CEO, and his or her compensation relative to that of the firm's second-highest-paid executive.

Finally, you need to look not only at what you and others are doing but also at what you aren't doing. The managers of one European investment bank told me that they measure performance by the outcomes of deals they've turned down as well as by the outcomes of deals they've won. If the ones they've rejected turn out to be lemons, those rejections count as successes. This kind of analysis seems obvious once stated, but I've noticed a persistent bias in all of us to focus on what we do over what we don't do. Good management is about making choices, so a decision not to do something should be analyzed as closely as a decision to do something.

Trap 3: Putting Your Faith in Numbers

Good or bad, the metrics in your performance assessment package all come as numbers. The problem is that numbers-driven managers often end up producing reams of low-quality data. Think about how companies collect feedback on service from their customers. It's well known to statisticians that if you want evaluation forms to tell the real story, the anonymity of the respondents must be protected. Yet out of a desire to gather as much information as possible at points of contact, companies routinely ask customers to include personal data, and in many cases the employees who provided the service watch them fill out the forms. How surprised should you be if your employees hand in consistently favorable forms that they themselves collected? Bad assessments have a tendency to mysteriously disappear.

Numbers-driven companies also gravitate toward the most popular measures. If they're looking to compare themselves with other companies, they feel they should use whatever measures others use. The question of what measure is the right one gets lost. Take Frederick Reichheld's widely used Net Promoter Score, which measures the likelihood that customers will recommend a product or service. The NPS is a useful indicator only if recommendations play the dominant role in a purchase decision; as its critics point out, customers' propensity to switch in response to recommendations varies from industry to industry, so an NPS is probably more important to, say, a baby-food manufacturer than to an electricity supplier.

Similar issues arise about the much touted link between employee satisfaction and profitability. The Employee-Customer-Profit Chain pioneered by Sears suggests that more-satisfied employees produce more-satisfied customers, who in turn deliver higher profits. If that's true, the path is clear: Keep your employees content and watch those profits soar. But employees may be satisfied mainly because they like their colleagues (think lawyers) or because they're highly paid and deferred to (think investment bankers). Or they may actually enjoy what they do, but their customers value price above the quality of service (think budget airlines).

A particular bugbear of mine is the application of financial metrics to nonfinancial activities. Anxious to justify themselves rather than be outsourced, many service functions (such as IT, HR, and legal) try to devise a return on investment number to help their cause. Indeed, ROI is often described as the holy grail of measurement—a revealing metaphor, with its implication of an almost certainly doomed search.

Suppose an HR manager undertakes to assign an ROI number to an executive training program. Typically, he or she would ask program participants to identify a benefit, assign a dollar value to it, and estimate the probability that the benefit came from the program. So a benefit that is worth $70,000 and has a 50% probability of being linked to the program means a program benefit of $35,000. If the program cost $25,000, the net benefit is $10,000—a 40% ROI.

Think about this for a minute. How on earth can the presumed causal link be justified? By a statement like "I learned a production algorithm at the program and then applied it"? Assessing any serious executive program requires a much more sophisticated and qualitative approach. First you have to specify ahead of time the needs of the program's stakeholders—participants, line managers, and sponsors—and make sure that the syllabus meets your organizational and talent management objectives. Once the program has ended, you have to look beyond immediate evaluations to at least six months after participants return to the workplace; their personal feedback should be incorporated in the next annual company performance review. At the soft drinks company Britvic, HR assesses its executive coaching program by tracking coachees for a year afterward, comparing their career trajectories with those of people who didn't get coached.

Trap 4: Gaming Your Metrics

In 2002 a leaked internal memo from associates at Clifford Chance, one of the world's largest law firms, contended that pressure to deliver billable hours had encouraged its lawyers to pad their numbers and created an incentive to allocate to senior associates work that could be done by less expensive junior associates.

Lawyers aren't the only ones: A number of prominent companies have been caught trying to manipulate their numbers. Since 2004 Royal Dutch Shell has paid $470 million to settle lawsuits relating to its overstatement of reserves. Morgan Stanley was reportedly willing to lose €20 million on a securities trade for the Finnish government just before closing its books for 2004 in order to improve its position in the league table for global equity capital market rankings.

You can't prevent people from gaming numbers, no matter how outstanding your organization. The moment you choose to manage by a metric, you invite your managers to manipulate it. Metrics are only proxies for performance. Someone who has learned how to optimize a metric without actually having to perform will often do just that. To create an effective performance measurement system, you have to work with that fact rather than resort to wishful thinking and denial.

It helps to diversify your metrics, because it's a lot harder to game several of them at once. Clifford Chance replaced its single metric of billable hours with seven criteria on which to base bonuses: respect and mentoring, quality of work, excellence in client service, integrity, contribution to the community, commitment to diversity, and contribution to the firm as an institution. Metrics should have varying sources (colleagues, bosses, customers) and time frames. Mehrdad Baghai and coauthors described in "Performance Measures: Calibrating for Growth" (*Journal of Business Strategy,* July–August 1999) how the Japanese telecommunications company SoftBank measured performance along three time horizons. Horizon 1 covered actions relevant to extending and defending core businesses, and metrics were based on current income and cash flow statements. Horizon 2 covered actions taken to build emerging businesses; metrics came from sales and marketing numbers. Horizon 3 covered creating opportunities for new businesses; success was measured through the attainment of preestablished milestones. Multiple levels like those make gaming far more complicated and far less likely to succeed.

You can also vary the boundaries of your measurement, by defining responsibility more narrowly or by broadening it. To reduce delays in gate-closing time, Southwest Airlines, which had traditionally applied a metric only to gate agents, extended it to include the whole ground team—ticketing staff, gate staff, and loaders—so that everyone had an incentive to cooperate.

Finally, you should loosen the link between meeting budgets and performance; far too many bonuses are awarded on that basis. Managers may either pad their budgets to make meeting them easier or pare them down too far to impress their bosses. Both practices can destroy value. Some companies get around the problem by giving managers leeway. The office supplier Staples, for example, lets them exceed their budgets if they can demonstrate that doing so will lead to improved service for customers. When I was a CFO, I offered scope for budget revisions during the year, usually in months three and six. Another way of providing budget flexibility is to set ranges rather than specific numbers as targets.

Trap 5: Sticking to Your Numbers Too Long

As the saying goes, you manage what you measure. Unfortunately, performance assessment systems seldom evolve as fast as businesses do. Smaller and growing companies are especially likely to fall into this trap. In the earliest stages, performance is all about survival, cash resources, and growth. Comparisons are to last week, last month, and last year. But as the business matures, the focus has to move to profit and the comparisons to competitors.

It's easy to spot the need for change after things have gone wrong, but how can you evaluate your measures before they fail you? The answer is to be very precise about what you want to assess, be explicit about what metrics are assessing it, and make sure that everyone is clear about both.

In looking for a measure of customer satisfaction, the British law firm Addleshaw Booth (now Addleshaw Goddard) discovered from a survey that its clients valued responsiveness most, followed by proactiveness and commercial-mindedness. Most firms would interpret this finding to mean they needed to be as quick as possible. Addleshaw Booth's managers dug deeper into the data to understand more exactly what "responsiveness" meant. What they found was that they needed to differentiate between clients. "One size does not fit all," an employee told me. "Being responsive for some clients means coming back to them in two hours; for others, it's 10 minutes."

The point is that if you specify the indicator precisely and loudly, everyone can more easily see when it's not fit for the purpose. The credit-rating agencies have come under attack because they gave AAA ratings to so many borrowers who turned out to be bad risks. The agencies have argued in their own defense that lenders misunderstood what the ratings meant. The AAA rating, they claim, was awarded on the basis of borrowers' credit records, and it described the likelihood of default under normal market conditions; it did not factor in what might happen in the event of a massive shock to the financial system. Reasonable as this explanation may be, it is no consolation to those who thought they knew what the magic AAA represented.

Why do organizations that excel in so many other ways fall into these traps? Because the people managing performance frameworks are generally not experts in performance measurement. Finance managers are proficient at tracking expenses, monitoring risks, and raising capital, but they seldom have a grasp of how operating realities connect with performance. They are precisely the people who strive to reduce judgments to a single ROI number. The people who understand performance are line managers—who, of course, are crippled by conflicts of interest.

A really good assessment system must bring finance and line managers into some kind of meaningful dialogue that allows the company to benefit from both the relative independence of the former and the expertise of the latter. This sounds straightforward enough, but as anyone who's ever worked in a real business knows, actually doing it is a rather tall order. Then again, who says the CEO's job is supposed to be easy?

Andrew Likierman is the dean of London Business School, a nonexecutive director of Barclays Bank, and the chairman of the UK's National Audit Office.

Finance Quiz

How Much Have You Learned?

Now it's time to retake the finance quiz that appeared in the first part of this guide. It will give you an indication of what you've learned and what you might need to study up on. The answers follow.

1. **The income statement measures:**
   a. Profitability
   b. Assets and liabilities
   c. Cash
   d. All of the above

2. **A sale on credit ends up on the income statement as revenue and as what on the balance sheet?**
   a. Accounts receivable
   b. Long-term assets
   c. Short-term liability
   d. Operating cash flow

3. **What happens when a company is profitable but collection lags behind payments to vendors?**
   a. The company is OK because profits always become cash
   b. The company stands a good chance of running out of money
   c. The company needs to shift its focus to EBIT
   d. The cash flow statement will show a negative bottom line

4. **How is gross profit margin calculated?**
   a. COGS/revenue
   b. Gross profit/net profit
   c. Gross profit/revenue
   d. Sales/gross profit

5. **Which statement summarizes changes to parts of the balance sheet?**
   a. Income statement
   b. Cash flow statement
   c. Neither of the above
   d. Both of the above

6. **EBIT is an important measure in companies because:**
   a. It is free cash flow
   b. It subtracts interest and taxes from net income to get a truer picture of the business
   c. It indicates the profitability of a company's operations
   d. It is the key measure of earnings before indirect costs and transfers

7. **Operating expenses include all of the following except:**
   a. Advertising costs
   b. Administrative salaries
   c. Expensed research and development costs
   d. Delivery of raw materials

8. **Owners' equity in a company increases when the company:**
   a. Increases its assets with debt
   b. Decreases its debt by paying off loans with company cash
   c. Increases its profit
   d. All of the above

9. **A company has more cash today when:**
   a. Customers pay their bills sooner
   b. Accounts receivable increases
   c. Profit increases
   d. Retained earnings increases

10. **Which of the following is not part of working capital?**
    a. Accounts receivable
    b. Inventory
    c. Property, plant, and equipment
    d. All of the above are part of working capital

Answers to the Finance Quiz

1. **a.** Profitability is measured by the income statement. Assets and liabilities are measured

by the balance sheet, cash by the cash flow statement.

2. **a.** A sale on credit means that the customer owes you for the amount of the purchase. That debt is an asset, and it appears under accounts receivable on the balance sheet.

3. **b.** If you're not collecting receivables as fast as you are paying vendors, you will need more and more working capital as the company grows—and if you can't find it, you will run out of money. EBIT is just another measure of profitability, which doesn't determine cash flow. And the cash flow statement's bottom line depends on many factors, not just receivables and payables.

4. **c.** Gross profit is revenue minus COGS (cost of goods sold). Gross profit margin shows gross profit as a percentage of revenue, so just divide gross profit by revenue and convert to a percent.

5. **d.** On the income statement, net profit adds to the retained earnings line on the balance sheet after dividends are paid. On the cash flow statement, the line items reflect cash-related differences between two balance sheets. Both statements thus summarize changes to the balance sheet.

6. **c.** EBIT, or operating profit, shows a company's profitability without regard to how the

company is financed (which affects interest expense) or the taxes it may owe. EBIT is not free cash flow. And it actually adds back in interest and taxes to get that picture of operating profitability. EBIT does not stand for earnings before indirect costs and transfers.

7. **d.** Delivery of raw materials is part of COGS (cost of goods sold), not operating expenses. Advertising, administrative, and expensed research and development costs are all operating expenses.

8. **c.** One element of owners' equity is retained earnings, meaning profits not distributed to shareholders as dividends. Increasing profits helps to build owners' equity through the retained earnings line. Using cash to pay debt or increasing debt and adding assets with that debt does not change equity.

9. **a.** It isn't until the customer actually pays its bill that a company's cash increases. Accounts receivable indicates future cash flows, not current ones. Neither profit nor retained earnings affects how soon a company gets its cash.

10. **c.** Working capital is current assets minus current liabilities. Property, plant, and equipment is not a current asset; rather, it represents long-term investments in the business.

Glossary

Accounts Payable. A category of balance-sheet liabilities representing funds owed by the company to suppliers and other short-term creditors.

Accounts Receivable. A category of balance-sheet assets representing funds owed to the company by customers and others.

Accrual Accounting. An accounting practice that records transactions as they occur, whether or not cash trades hands.

Allocations. See **indirect costs.**

Assets. The balance-sheet items in which a company invests so that it can conduct business. Examples include cash and financial instruments, inventories of raw materials and finished goods, land, buildings, and equipment.

Adapted from *Harvard Business Essentials: Finance for Managers* (product #8768), Harvard Business Review Press, 2002

Assets also include funds owed to the company by customers and others—an asset category referred to as **accounts receivable.**

Balance Sheet. A financial statement that describes the assets owned by the business and how those assets are financed—with the funds of creditors (liabilities), the equity of the owners, or both. Also known as the **statement of financial position.**

Book Value of Shareholder Equity. A balance-sheet valuation method that calculates value as total assets less total liabilities.

Breakeven Analysis. A form of analysis that helps determine how much (or how much more) a company needs to sell in order to pay for the fixed investment—in other words, at what point the company will break even on its cash flow.

Budget. A document that translates strategic plans into measurable quantities that express the expected resources required and anticipated returns over a certain period. It functions as an action plan and presents the estimated future financial statements of the organization.

Burden. See **indirect costs.**

Cash Flow Statement. A financial statement that details the reasons for changes in cash (and cash equivalents) during the accounting period. More specifically, it reflects all changes in cash relating to operating activities, investments, and financing.

Common Stock. A security that represents a fractional ownership interest in the corporation that issued it.

Contribution Margin. In cost accounting, the contribution by each unit of production to overhead and profits, or net revenue less direct cost per unit.

Cost/Benefit Analysis. A form of analysis that evaluates whether, over a given time frame, the benefits of a new investment or business opportunity will outweigh the associated costs.

Cost of Capital. The opportunity cost that shareholders and lenders could earn on their capital if they invested in the next-best opportunity available to them at the same level of risk, calculated as the weighted average cost of the organization's different sources of capital.

Cost of Goods Sold (COGS). On the income statement, what it costs a company to produce its goods and services. This figure at a minimum includes raw materials and direct labor costs.

Current Assets. Assets that are most easily converted to cash: cash, cash equivalents such as certificates of deposit and U.S. Treasury bills, receivables, and inventory. Under generally accepted accounting principles, current assets are those that can be converted into cash within one year.

Current Liabilities. Liabilities that must be paid in a year or less; these typically include short-term loans, salaries, income taxes, and accounts payable.

Current Ratio. Current assets divided by current liabilities. This ratio is often used as a measure of a company's ability to meet currently maturing obligations.

Days Receivables Outstanding. The average time it takes to collect on sales.

Debt Ratio. The ratio of debt to either assets or equity in a company's financial structure.

Depreciation. A noncash charge that effectively reduces the balance sheet value of an asset over its useful life.

Direct Costs. Cost incurred as a direct consequence of producing a good or service—as opposed to overhead, or indirect costs.

Discounted Cash Flow (DCF). A method based on time-value-of-money concepts that calculates value by finding the present value of a business's future cash flows.

Discount Rate. The annual rate, expressed as a percentage, at which a future payment or series of payments is reduced to its present value.

Dividend. A distribution of after-tax corporate earnings to shareholders.

Earnings Before Interest and Taxes (EBIT). See **operating earnings.**

Earnings Per Share (EPS). A company's net earnings divided by the total number of shares outstanding.

Economic Value Added (EVA). A measure of real economic profit calculated as net operating income after tax less the cost of the capital employed to obtain it.

Equity Book Value. The value of total assets less total liabilities.

Financial Leverage. The degree to which borrowed money is used in acquiring assets. A corporation is said to be highly leveraged when its balance-sheet debt is much greater than its owners' equity.

Fixed Assets. Assets that are difficult to convert to cash—for example, buildings and equipment. Sometimes called **plant assets.**

Future Value (FV). The amount to which a present value, or series of payments, will increase over a specific period at a specific compounding rate.

Generally Accepted Accounting Principles (GAAP). In the United States, a body of conventions, rules, and procedures sanctioned by the Financial Accounting Standards Board, an independent, self-regulating body. All entities must follow GAAP in accounting for transactions and representing their results in financial statements.

Goodwill. If a company has purchased another company for a price in excess of the fair market value of its assets, that "goodwill" is recorded on the balance sheet as an asset. Goodwill may represent intangible things such as the acquired company's reputation, its customer list, its brand names, and its patents.

Gross Profit Margin. Sales revenue less cost of goods sold, expressed as a percentage of revenue. The roughest measure of profitability. Also referred to as **gross margin.**

Hurdle Rate. The minimal rate of return that all investments for a particular enterprise must achieve.

Income Statement. A financial statement that indicates the cumulative financial results of operations over a specified period. Also referred to as the **profit-and-loss statement,** or **P&L.**

Indirect Costs. Costs that cannot be attributed to the production of any particular unit of output. Often referred to as **overhead, allocations,** or **burden.**

Interest Coverage Ratio. Earnings before interest and taxes divided by interest expense. Creditors use this ratio to gauge a company's ability to make future interest payments in the face of fluctuating operating results.

Internal Rate of Return (IRR). The discount rate at which the net present value of an investment equals zero.

Inventory. The supplies, raw materials, components, and so forth, that a company uses in its operations. It also includes work in process—goods in various stages of production—as well as finished goods waiting to be sold and/or shipped.

Inventory Turnover. Cost of goods sold divided by average inventory.

Liability. A claim against a company's assets.

Liquidity. The extent to which a company's assets can readily be turned into cash for meeting incoming obligations.

Net Earnings. See **net income.**

Net Income. The "bottom line" of the income statement. Net income is revenues less expenses less taxes. Also referred to as **net earnings** or **net profits.**

Net Present Value (NPV). The present value of one or more future cash flows less any initial investment costs.

Net Profits. See **net income.**

Net Working Capital. Current assets less current liabilities; the amount of money a company has tied up in short-term operating activities.

Operating Budget. A projected target for performance in revenues, expenses, and operating income.

Operating Earnings. On the income statement, gross margin less operating expenses and depreciation. Often called **earnings before interest and taxes,** or **EBIT.**

Operating Expense. On the income statement, a category that includes administrative expenses, employee salaries, rents, sales and marketing costs, and other costs of business not directly attributed to the cost of manufacturing a product.

Operating Leverage. The extent to which a company's operating costs are fixed versus variable. For example, a company that relies heavily on machinery and uses very few workers to produce its goods has a high operating leverage.

Operating Margin. A financial ratio used by many analysts to gauge the profitability of a company's operating activities. It is calculated as earnings before interest and taxes (EBIT) divided by net sales.

Overhead. See **indirect costs.**

Owners' Equity. What, if anything, is left over after total liabilities are deducted from total assets. Owners' equity is the sum of capital contributed by owners plus the company's total retained earnings over time. Also known as **shareholders' equity.**

Payback Period. The length of time it will take a particular investment to pay for itself.

Plant Assets. See **fixed assets.**

Present Value (PV). The monetary value today of a future payment discounted at some annual compound interest rate.

Profit-and-Loss Statement (P&L). See **income statement.**

Profit Margin. The percentage of every dollar of sales that makes it to the bottom line. Profit margin is net income after tax divided by net sales. Sometimes called **return on sales,** or **ROS.**

Retained Earnings. Annual net profits left after payment of dividends that accumulate on a company's balance sheet.

Return on Assets (ROA). Relates net income to the company's total asset base and is calculated as net income divided by total assets.

Return on Equity (ROE). Relates net income to the amount invested by shareholders (both initially and through retained earnings). It is a measure of the productivity of the shareholders' stake in the business and is calculated as net income divided by shareholders' equity.

Return on Sales (ROS). See **profit margin.**

Revenue. The amount of money that results from selling products or services to customers.

Shareholders' Equity. See **owners' equity**.

Solvency. A situation in which a company's assets outweigh its liabilities—that is, owners' equity is positive.

Statement of Financial Position. See **balance sheet**.

Variance. The difference between actual and expected results in the budget. A variance can be favorable, when the actual results are better than expected, or unfavorable, when the actual results are worse than expected.

Working Capital. See **net working capital**.

Index

Notes

Notes

Notes

Notes